Knock Knock

A COMEDY IN THREE ACTS

by Jules Feiffer

SAMUEL FRENCH, INC.

25 WEST 45TH STREET   NEW YORK 10036
7623 SUNSET BOULEVARD   HOLLYWOOD 90046
LONDON   *TORONTO*

OPENING NIGHT FEBRUARY 24, 1976
BILTMORE THEATRE

TERRY ALLEN KRAMER and HARRY RIGBY
by arrangement with CIRCLE REPERTORY COMPANY

present

JULES FEIFFER'S
new comedy

KNOCK KNOCK

Directed by

MARSHALL W. MASON

with

NEIL	JUDD	DANIEL	NANCY
FLANAGAN	HIRSCH	SELTZER	SNYDER

Costumes by
JENNIFER VON MAYRHAUSER

Setting by　　　　　*Lighting by*
JOHN LEE BEATTY　　**DENNIS PARICHY**

Sound by
CHARLES LONDON and GEORGE HANSEN

CAST
(in order of appearance)

Cohn . . . . DANIEL SELTZER
Abe . . . . NEIL FLANAGAN
Wiseman . . . . JUDD HIRSCH
Joan . . . . NANCY SNYDER
Messenger, Gambler, Judge . . . . JUDD HIRSCH

JOAN'S VOICES ARE PLAYED by JUDD HIRSCH

The time is the present—The place is a small house in the woods.

CHARACTERS

Cohn

Abe

Wiseman

Joan

First Voice

Second Voice

4

Knock Knock

ACT ONE

SCENE 1

The time is the present. A small log house in the woods. It is unpainted, cramped, containing the worldly goods of two lifetimes, COHN's and ABE's. Books and periodicals litter every surface including the floor, which is covered with an old Persian rug. Two out-of-use TVs, circa 1950. An aged radio-phonograph console, next to it on the floor a stack of classical LPs. A large oak table that serves as a dining table and ABE's desk. A typewriter, holding a blank sheet of paper at ABE's end of the table; next to it a ream of blank paper. The kitchen is separated from the living-dining room by a tattered screen, covered with magazine cutouts of famous faces: Einstein, Tolstoy, Beethoven, Toscanini, F.D.R., Gandhi, Joe Louis, Babe Ruth, Katharine Cornell . . . The kitchen is well-equipped: a huge iron range, shelves of spices, canned goods, other supplies. A shelf of cookbooks. Two burlap contained doorways lead to the bedrooms. A tiny windowed door leads outside. The view through two dark windows is of vegetation: crawling vines, blackened leaves. Pictures bury the walls: simply framed, very small, mostly family photographs and postcard-size reproductions of impressionist paintings. Near the fireplace: a large steamer trunk. Somewhere close to the kitchen: an open ironing board; on it a gray-

5

ing bundle of shirts, living there for days. On a side table: COHN'S violin, near it, a music stand. In addition to the two dining room chairs there is an old rocker: COHN'S, and a huge, beat up, over-stuffed armchair: ABE'S.

AT RISE: COHN, *overweight and 50, is at the stove reading from a cookbook and mixing ingredients into a pot. He is humming a Mozart aria. He hums, cooks, tastes. Across the room,* ABE, *under-weight and 50, lies in his chair, staring into space. He lights a cigar and meditates.*

ABE. It's getting better.

COHN. (*Tastes.*) Who says?

ABE. I say.

COHN. (*Mixes.*) With what evidence?

ABE. My eyes are my evidence?

COHN. (*Turns to* ABE *and raises two fingers.*) How many fingers?

ABE. Five.

COHN. Some eyes. (*Goes back to his cooking.*)

ABE. All right, two.

COHN. (*Slams down the pot and turns to* ABE.) So if you can see two, why do you say five?

ABE. I prefer five.

COHN. That's not a reason.

ABE. Why does there always have to be a reason?

COHN. Abe, I've known you for twenty-five years and for there's never a reason.

ABE. And you? You're better off.

COHN. I don't invent.

ABE. I beg your pardon. Neither do I.

COHN. What kind of fool am I living with? You just made up five.

ABE. I didn't make it up.

COHN. Not a minute ago.

ABE. No.

COHN. I was holding up two (*Holds up two fingers.*) and you said I was holding up five! (*Holds up five fingers.*)

ABE. You *are* holding up five.

COHN. (*He quickly puts down his hand.*) What's the use?

ABE. Cohn, I'll tell you something—you're rigid. I'm flexible.

COHN. Mindless.

ABE. You only believe in what's in front of your nose. That's not mindless?

COHN. I don't make things up.

ABE. (*Points to curtained doorway.*) What's that?

COHN. Don't bother me. (ABE *continues to point.*) It's my bedroom! (*Goes back to his cooking.*) Pest!

ABE. I don't see any bedroom.

COHN. You know it's my bedroom!

ABE. I beg your pardon. All I see is a curtain. (COHN *goes and pulls back the curtain.*) Ah hah! A bedroom! (ABE *rises, crosses to the doorway and pulls the curtain back into place.*) A curtain. (*Pulls the curtain back and forth.*) A bedroom. A curtain. A bedroom. A curtain. A bedroom. Is it still a bedroom when you don't see it?

COHN. It's always a bedroom!

ABE. So for you it's always a bedroom and for me it's always five fingers. (COHN *slams the plate down on the table, pours stew into it and begins to eat.* ABE *joins him at the table, studies the blank sheet in his typewriter, punches one key and nods seriously at the results.*) I'm right so I don't get any stew?

COHN. You want stew? Here! (*Hands him pot.*)

ABE. (*Looks into pot.*) It's empty.

COHN. (*Points to empty pot.*) What's that?

ABE. A pot.

COHN. You saw me cook stew in it? (ABE *nods.*) You saw me pour stew out of it? (ABE *nods.*) So eat your stew. (ABE, *unhappily, watches* COHN *eat.* COHN *wipes his mouth and points to the empty space in front of* ABE.) Eat! That's steak. That's potatoes. That's salad. That's beer. Hearty appetite!

ABE. That's vicious.

COHN. (*Smiles, self-satisfied.*) Abe, you can pull the wool over your eyes but you can't pull it over mine. I know you every step of the way. I know you inside and out.

ABE. I'm hungry.

COHN. So make something.

ABE. You know I don't cook. I burn everything.

COHN. Don't.

ABE. My mind wanders. (COHN *gets up, crosses to stock shelf, takes down a box of spaghetti, sets a plate in front of* ABE *and pours the uncooked spaghetti into the plate.*) It's not cooked.

COHN. I say it's cooked. Two fingers. Five fingers. Eat your spaghetti. (ABE *looks disconsolately at the plate, picks the spaghetti sticks up in his hand and begins to eat them.* COHN *watches for a moment, then relents. He takes the plate away from* ABE *and pours the spaghetti into a pot of water on the stove.*) When will you learn?

ABE. To be like you? I beg your pardon, is that such a blessing?

COHN. Don't get personal.

ABE. I don't like being made a fool of.

COHN. You asked for it.

ABE. I know I'm right. (COHN *groans.*) You can win the argument but it doesn't mean you're right. Inside I know who's right.

COHN. You think so?

ABE. I know so. With my ex-wife, I also lost all arguments. But you told me I was right.

COHN. With her you *were* right.

ABE. So if I lost with her and was right, you have to admit that when I lose with you I also could be right. It's consistent.

COHN. Abe, I'm going to tell you a little story. A parable. After I finish you tell me what it means to you. OK?

ABE. Before I eat?

COHN. Here. (*Cuts him a slice of cheese.* ABE *wolfs it down.*) Once there was this beautiful, innocent, young maid, golden locks, of eighteen who lived in a dark forest in the country with her very proud, strict parents and it was her habit to sit by a pond day in and day out and moan and mope about the moment when love would first enter her life. One day this lovely young thing is daydreaming by the pond when a frog hops out of the water and into her lap. The beautiful maid recoils. "Don't be frightened" croaks the ugly little frog, "I am not what I appear to be. I am in truth a handsome young Prince cast under a spell by a wicked witch and this spell can only be broken when some fair maid takes me into her bed and spends the night by my side." So the girl calmed down and decided why not? So she brought the frog home and she took it to bed with her and the next morning she woke up—and lying next to her was this tall, handsome, naked young Prince. And that's the way she explained it to her parents when they walked in on the two of them. What's the moral of the story?

ABE. The moral is you're a very cynical man.

COHN. You want dinner? Then discuss it intelligently.

ABE. (*Leaves the table and returns to his own chair.*) The moral is you take a classic fable with charm and beauty that deals with dreams and imagination and you change it into men's room humor. That's the moral. What you reveal of yourself. (*Leaves his chair, crosses to the typewriter, punches a key and sits back down again.*)

COHN. You would believe the girl's story?

ABE. I beg your pardon, I wouldn't be her prosecutor. I leave that to you.

COHN. Supposing you're the girl's father?

ABE. I would face the problem with compassion.

COHN. First admitting it's a problem!

ABE. A man in bed with my daughter? At first—until the situation's cleared up, I have to admit it's a problem.

COHN. Then she tells you the story of the frog.

ABE. Which clears up everything.

COHN. You believe about the frog?

ABE. What's important is she believes about the frog. We didn't bring her up to lie.

COHN. You'd rather have her crazy than lie.

ABE. Why is that crazy?

COHN. Or hallucinating.

ABE. Because her mind can conjure with change—with ugliness turning into beauty—you call that hallucinating? And what *you* see—only beauty turning into ugliness—you call that reality? I beg your pardon, Cohn, you're living in a stacked deck. You give me a choice, I prefer frogs into Princes over Princes into frogs.

COHN. Even if it's not so.

ABE. How do we know? All I'm saying is we don't know.

COHN. Do we know that you're Abe and I'm Cohn?

ABE. In this life.

COHN. In this life. But in another life maybe I was Abe and you were Cohn.

ABE. It's possible. Anything's possible.

COHN. Or that I was Mozart and you were Thomas Jefferson?

ABE. It's unlikely. But it's possible.

COHN. Or that I was Moses and you were Christ.

ABE. It's possible.

COHN. Abe, I'm going to give you a chance to listen to what you just said: It's possible you were Christ.

ABE. I didn't say probable. I said possible.

COHN. And it's possible that if I rub this lamp a genie will come out?

ABE. All I'm saying is we don't know, do we?

COHN. (*He rubs the lamp.*) Now we know.

ABE. I beg your pardon, we know about one lamp. We don't know about all lamps. Also we don't know that a genie *didn't* come out. We don't know that there isn't a genie in this room this very moment. And that he isn't saying "Master, I am the genie of the lamp and I have three wishes to grant you and anything you wish will come true." Maybe he's there and maybe we've been taught how not to see genies in our time. Or hear them. Or take advantage when they offer us three wishes. That's all I'm saying. That it could be us, not him.

COHN. Who?

ABE. The genie.

COHN. Abe, if I had three wishes you know what would be my first wish? That instead of you to talk to, to drive me crazy for another twenty years, I had somebody with a brain I could talk to! That's what I wish!

(*A sudden explosion engulfs* ABE. *Light and music effects. The smoke clears and sitting in his place is a bearded* WISEMAN *in robes. He holds a clipboard and a pen.*)

WISEMAN. Name?!

COHN. (*Shaken.*) Cohn.

WISEMAN. (*Checks the clipboard.*) That's right—Cohn. Occupation?!

COHN. Musician.

WISEMAN. (*Smiles.*) Musician. Where are you a musician, Cohn?

COHN. At the present I am unemployed.

WISEMAN. (*Smiles.*) At the present you are unemployed, is that right, Cohn?

COHN. Yes.

WISEMAN. At the present—let me see if I have this straight—you are an unemployed musician.

COHN. That's right.

WISEMAN. Unemployed. But still a musician.

COHN. Yes.

WISEMAN. What are you first, Cohn? A musician or an unemployed?

COHN. I don't understand the question.

WISEMAN. You wanted someone intelligent to talk to?

COHN. Yes.

WISEMAN. Meaning that he will be on your level. That's what you mean by intelligent, isn't it, Cohn? (*Waits.*) Well? Isn't it?

COHN. I guess it is.

WISEMAN. By that we are to assume that you consider yourself intelligent. Or do I go too far, Cohn?

COHN. No.

WISEMAN. No what?

COHN. What you said.

WISEMAN. That I go too far?

COHN. (*Inaudible.*) No.

WISEMAN. I can't hear you.

COHN. The other—what else you said first.

WISEMAN. That you consider yourself—don't let me put words in your mouth—intelligent. Though unemployed, out of work, a ward of the State, you consider yourself intelligent. And that you want as a companion—am I right in this?—someone of equal intelligence. I am not putting words in your mouth?

COHN. No. Equal intelligence. That's it.

WISEMAN. You want another unemployed musician?

COHN. Look—what's happened to Abe?

WISEMAN. Who?

COHN. Abe—my friend.

WISEMAN. You want Abe?

COHN. I want to know where he went.

WISEMAN. You miss this Abe? Is he another unemployed musician?

COHN. A stockbroker. Mutual funds. Retired.

WISEMAN. A wealthy retired stockbroker.

COHN. Yes.

WISEMAN. Supporting you?

COHN. He was sitting in that chair.

WISEMAN. In my chair?

COHN. It's Abe's chair.

WISEMAN. It's Wiseman's chair.

COHN. Who?

WISEMAN. Myself. Helmut Wiseman. It is my chair. You see? I am sitting in it. See how I sit in it, relax in it, lean back in it? So whose chair would you say this is? Does it look as if I've been out of this chair? Conversely, does it not look as if I have always been in this chair? How tall is this Abe?

COHN. Five foot eight.

WISEMAN. He is too short for this chair. You either have the wrong man or the wrong chair. Or the wrong height. If you had another height you might have the right man. But it would still be the wrong chair. No, I'm sorry, I can't help you. This is my chair. I, Wiseman. Mine. I know—you must have the wrong house! Try next door.

COHN. This is my house.

WISEMAN. (*He refers to his clipboard.*) Whose?

COHN. (*Quickly.*) Abe's. Abe and I live here.

WISEMAN. In this house?

COHN. Yes!

WISEMAN. Or a house very much like this?

COHN. It's *this* house!

WISEMAN. It can't be this house because it's not the right chair.

COHN. It *is* the right chair!

WISEMAN. Then why isn't Abe sitting here? You

see, Cohn, your argument collapses of its own weight. I'm sorry, I would like to spend more time with you but there are others waiting. Will you send in the next applicant, please?

COHN. What?

WISEMAN. (*Points to door.*) On your way out will you send in the next applicant? (*A knock on the door.*) You see, they are getting impatient.

COHN. This is *my* house!

WISEMAN. Your house? Well, I like that! Now you see here, Mr. Wiseman—

COHN. You're *Wiseman!*

WISEMAN. (*Indignant.*) Oh! And I suppose I'm Cohn!

COHN. *I'm* Cohn!

WISEMAN. Now *you're* Cohn. It's your chair, your house and your Cohn. Then who am I, may I ask?

COHN. I don't know who you are! You barge in here—

WISEMAN. Barge in? Did you see me barge in?

COHN. In a manner of speaking.

WISEMAN. No, I'm sorry, Mr. Wiseman or whatever you call yourself, I don't at all care for your manner of speaking. Your manner of speaking is offensive to me. Now if you had a nicer manner of speaking, something like: (*Sweet voiced.*) "Hello. How are you? I like you. Will you be my friend?" Well, that would be another manner entirely. But the way things stand now, the position is already filled. (*Knock on door.*) And tell the others to come back tomorrow. I'm going to bed. (WISEMAN *rises and disappears behind the curtained doorway leading into* COHN'S *bedroom.*) —A terrible day. I want to leave a call for seven. (COHN *crosses to the doorway.*) If you don't have seven in stock, make it nine. (*Another knock.* COHN *turns to the door.*)

COHN. Who—who's there?

JOAN. Joan.

COHN. Joan who?

JOAN. (*Sings.*) Joan no why there's no sun up in the sky, stormy weather.

COHN. (*He growls and grabs the poker from the fireplace.*) Enough's enough! (*To* JOAN.) Did you hear? Enough is enough!

WISEMAN. Will you kids quiet it down in there?

COHN. (*Whirls toward bedroom.*) Wiseman!! (*Advances on bedroom with poker.*) I warn you I'm armed!! (*He disappears behind the curtain. Sounds of a fight. Violent curtain moves. After a moment* WISEMAN *skips out, opens the refrigerator, takes out a carrot and skips back. Throughout* WISEMAN'S *exit and return the sound of the fight and the bustling of the curtain continue. A moment later,* COHN *crawls out of the bedroom, his clothes in tatters. He throws open the trunk in the corner and pulls out a shotgun. He crawls back inside with the shotgun. A loud blast.* COHN *staggers out, dragging the dead* WISEMAN. *A door knock.* COHN *freezes, holding* WISEMAN.) Who's there?

JOAN. Joan.

COHN. Joan who?

JOAN. Joan ask me no questions and I'll tell you no lies.

(COHN *drags* WISEMAN *over to the trunk and with great difficulty manages to squeeze him into it. But not all of him. He pushes down on the head and the legs pop out. He sticks the legs back in and the head and shoulders slide up. This goes on for a while until finally all of* WISEMAN *is in the trunk and* COHN *slams shut the lid, at which point the side collapses and* WISEMAN'S *legs pop out.* COHN *stares sullenly at* WISEMAN'S *exposed legs. Another knock.*)

COHN. (*Wearily*.) Joan who?

JOAN. (*Sings*.) Joan sit under the apple tree with anyone else but me.

COHN. I thought so. (*He folds back the edge of the rug, slides the trunk next to it, then unfolds the rug over* WISEMAN'S *legs. He skulks back into the bedroom and comes out with the shotgun. He crosses to the door and listens. During the above we hear the following through the door.*)

JOAN. He won't let me in.

FIRST VOICE. He has to!

SECOND VOICE. Did you tell him who you are?

JOAN. No.

FIRST VOICE. Tell him.

JOAN. I can't.

SECOND VOICE. Why not?

JOAN. It sounds like name-dropping.

FIRST VOICE. Maybe he hasn't heard of you.

JOAN. He must have heard of me.

SECOND VOICE. How do you know if you don't tell him. (*Pause*.)

JOAN. Knock. Knock.

COHN. (*Reloads shotgun*.) Who's there?

JOAN. Joan.

COHN. (*Getting ready*.) Joan who?

JOAN. Joan of Arc. (COHN *whips open the door and blasts away. A loud clang.* COHN *recoils in horror, drops the gun and backs off. In walks a vision of loveliness wearing a suit of armor. The breastplate has a big black dent in it.* JOAN *glares at* COHN, *crosses herself and starts talking to her body*.) Are you all right?

FIRST VOICE. I'm all right—a little shaky.

SECOND VOICE. I'm upset but I'm all right.

COHN. (*Gasping*.) Who are you?

FIRST VOICE. That's some greeting.

SECOND VOICE. You got any more surprises like that?

COHN. Who are they?

JOAN. (*Taps the dent in her armor.*) My voices. (COHN *retreats to the curtained doorway, turns quickly and throws the shotgun into the bedroom, then turns back to* JOAN.)

COHN. I'm not a violent man— (*A loud blast from the bedroom.* COHN *ducks his head behind the curtain and out again.*)

FIRST VOICE. He's a pacifist.

SECOND VOICE. I'd like to pacifist *him* right in the mouth.

COHN. No harm done. Has this been a day! Look— (*Slowly regaining confidence through the sound of his own voice.*) Certain things we know. I'll make myself clear. We know that maturity is the weaning out of synthetics in one's life, so that where in one's childhood one's life was a will-o'-the-wisp fantasy-laden, hodgepodge, over the years it develops into a spare, clear-eyed, precise, concise, essentially organic whole. Ask questions. I'm not a pedant.

JOAN. You think life is a hole. Life is holy, not a hole.

COHN. An organic whole. (*Indicates with motion of his hand.*)

JOAN. Small wonder you go around shooting people. You don't know what's important.

COHN. I don't shoot people.

FIRST VOICE. You want to know where the hole is?

SECOND VOICE. In your head!

COHN. Look— (*A long exasperated pause.*) Who are they?

JOAN. My voices? (COHN *nods.*) They're my voices.

COHN. (*Restraining himself.*) What have you got inside there? A tape recorder?

JOAN. (*Crosses herself.*) You pitiful man. (*Places a hand on his shoulder.*) We must be on our way. Are these rags all you own?

COHN. I don't leave here.

JOAN. But you must come with me—

COHN. No!

JOAN. To see the Emperor!

COHN. Emperor— (*Quickly back-pedals, and bangs into the trunk.* WISEMAN's *legs kick up in the air under the rug.*) I'll make a contribution— (*Reaches into his pocket.*)

JOAN. I want you!

COHN. I live here. I stay here. Take the trunk! It's a gift!

JOAN. My mission is to bring you, among others, before the Emperor. It is your duty to follow me.

COHN. (*Retreats behind curtain.*) You're barking up the wrong tree. I never leave here. Ask anyone. They never see me leave here. They don't know me. Ask anyone if they know me. They'll say "Who?"

JOAN. You must do as I say!

COHN. I have to go with you to see the Emperor. What Emperor? What for? To tell him the sky is falling?

JOAN. The sky is not falling.

COHN. (*Sarcastic.*) Thank God!

JOAN. It is missing.

COHN. (*Comes out from behind curtain with change of clothes.*) *What's* missing?

JOAN. The sky is missing! We must find the Emperor to give him the wonderful news that the sky is missing and that mankind's path to heaven is at last unblocked and unimpeded, and that God calls on His Highness, the Emperor, to build a thousand spaceships and put on them two of every kind and blast off for heaven. Before the holocaust.

COHN. (*Sits her down.*) OK. (*Pause.*) Let's take this a little bit at a time. First of all, there's an Emperor, right? (JOAN *nods.*) And he lives—where *does* he live? (JOAN *points.*) He lives that way. (JOAN *nods.*) And you are heading a delegation of citizens to petition the Emperor to build a spaceship—

JOAN. A thousand spaceships!

COHN. To take us to, you said heaven, am I right? (JOAN *nods*.) Because the sky which has always been up there is not up there any more. (JOAN *nods*.) In fact, it is missing. And we are to bring this piece of news to the Emperor, this man you call the Emperor. And he is to put two of every kind on spaceships—and thus save us from the holocaust. (JOAN *nods*.) And everybody else dies. We're saved. Everybody else dies. Is that a mission or is that a mission!

JOAN. Don't be dense: it has nothing to do with dying. It's more or less like moving. Some people live in the city and some people live in the suburbs and some people live in the country and some people live in heaven.

COHN. You don't have to die to go to heaven any more?

JOAN. Not since the sky is missing. You simply *move* there. But first, of course, you have to know it's there. For example, if your entire life were spent in the city would you know about cows and trees? No! Well, it's no different with heaven. True, we may know about it in a *religious* sense, but certainly not as a place to migrate.

COHN. (*With infinite patience.*) But isn't it cruel— maybe cruel is too strong a word—isn't it thoughtless to abandon everyone else to the holocaust?

JOAN. (*Brightly.*) I'm glad you asked me that question. I, too, thought it was cruel but my voices tell me that people will never know it's a holocaust. They'll adapt themselves. Many may even find happiness. (*Goes to door.*) Are you ready?

COHN. Young lady, sit down, I have some shocking news to break to you. (*He sits* JOAN *back down in a chair.*) There is no Emperor.

JOAN. You might as well say there is no God.

COHN. There is no God.

JOAN. You might as well say there is no me and there is no you.

COHN. There is a me; that's all I concede.

JOAN. But there is no me?

COHN. For your information, you are not Joan of Arc.

JOAN. And my voices?

COHN. There are no voices.

FIRST VOICE. There are too!

COHN. There are not!

SECOND VOICE. Are too! Are too!

COHN. Are not! Are not!

FIRST and SECOND VOICES. Are! Are! Are!

COHN. Not! Not! Not!

JOAN. Then whom are you arguing with?

COHN. (*Calms down.*) It's not an argument, just a discussion. I wish you'd tell me how you do that.

JOAN. Have you never believed in anything?

COHN. I believe in me. After that there's room for doubt.

JOAN. But it's so lonely!

COHN. That's my problem.

JOAN. How can you bear it?

COHN. If you're strong, you can bear what's true. If you're weak, you make up fairy tales.

JOAN. You think I make up fairy tales?

COHN. I'm not singling you out. Abe, my best friend. Him also. *He'd* go with you to see the Emperor. Not that he'd believe. He wouldn't believe. But just in case. With Abe it's always just in case. He's built an ethic out of "maybe," "who's to know," "just in case." (*In a rage.*) He has no convictions! *No convictions!* I much prefer someone crazy like you who thinks she's Joan of Arc. That at least is a position. So that's another reason. I have to stay in the house to take care of Abe; I can't go with you to see the Emperor.

JOAN. We'll take him with us!

COHN. He's not here.

JOAN. Where is he?

COHN. That's the question. Vanished! Vanished to annoy me. You watch. I'll pay him back good. We had an argument— I won't bore you with the details—but it got around—who knows how?—to wishes. Two grown men, an argument over wishes. Abe said it's possible I had three, I said baloney. Abe said I couldn't know unless I wished, so I wished Abe would stop bothering me and vanish, and to make a long story short, in order to aggravate me, he did.

JOAN. Wish him back.

COHN. If life were only so simple.

JOAN. The first wish worked.

COHN. A trick.

JOAN. Are you afraid?

COHN. (*Smiles.*) Afraid? Of what? Of wishes? Of voices? The only thing I'm afraid of is insanity. And that's a losing battle.

JOAN. I believe in your wishes!

COHN. That's reassuring.

JOAN. I do!

COHN. (*Shakes his head sadly.*) What do you know? Nothing. No background. I'll make a bet, no education. What do you have for credentials? Nothing!

FIRST and SECOND VOICES. *Us!*

COHN. Less than nothing!

JOAN. I was once very much like you.

COHN. (*Enraged.*) No one was ever like me! (*Calms himself.*) Don't be presumptuous.

JOAN. I was sad all the time.

COHN. I'm not sad.

JOAN. In despair.

COHN. This isn't despair.

JOAN. What do you call it?

COHN. Realism.

JOAN. Then why is it so much like despair?

COHN. I didn't say they're not connected. But they're not the same. With despair you feel there's no hope so you might as well die; with realism you feel there's no hope but you get a kick out of it.

JOAN. I wanted to die!

COHN. See? We're oceans apart.

JOAN. I lived in a sea of despair—

COHN. Not the same!

JOAN. —with my wicked stepmother and her three wicked daughters.

COHN. Wait. You're confused. That's Cinderella.

JOAN. Exactly.

COHN. You're Joan of Arc.

JOAN. Oh, I don't mean *now*.

COHN. You used to be Cinderella?

JOAN. Of course!

COHN. But now you're Joan or Arc? (JOAN *nods, patiently*.) Well, you're certainly working your way up in the world. Of course, instead of marrying Prince Charming you get burned at the stake, but you do make sainthood while all Cinderella gets is to live happily ever after. And in one case Shaw writes about you and in the other case, Walt Disney. All in all, I'd say you made a wise choice.

JOAN. Choice? What choice? After the ball, I thought the Prince loved me and I dreamed—well, no matter what I dreamed—he came looking for me, door to door, with a glass slipper. Like a salesman! . . . Can you imagine my shame? That he, my true love, would only know me by trying a shoe on my foot! I walked barefoot on rocks, soaked my feet in brine, anything to fail such a test. But it was never to be made. One door away from ours the Prince was suddenly called to war and I was left with a broken heart and a size nine foot. So I became a nun. A very poor nun. Night after night, visions of our Lord came to me bearing a glass slipper. So I fled the nunnery and travelled the land as a migrant fruit-picker. I married and begat five Portuguese children. My husband was a sot and beat me. When my children grew of age, they beat me.

So I threw myself off a bridge, into the river. I landed on my feet and, to my considerable surprise, saw that I was standing on the water. I walked on the water for miles trying to decipher the meaning of my fate. Half-mad with the complexities of it all, I tried again to drown myself; this time by standing on my head and ducking it under the water. But the further under I ducked, the more the water level receded, until finally, the river ran dry. I knew that it was a sign! I fell to my knees and prayed God for His forgiveness and that I should prove myself worthy of being His servant. And on the fortieth day my voices came and told me who I was and what I must do. And now, praise God, I am Joan and I am here!

COHN. (*Stares at her. After a long silence.*) I really miss Abe.

JOAN. You don't believe my story.

COHN. You can walk on water, bring back Abe.

JOAN. Voices? May I?

FIRST VOICE. He shoots us and then he wants favors.

SECOND VOICE. He's got two more wishes. Why come to us?

JOAN. You *can* wish him back.

COHN. Oy.

JOAN. You can.

COHN. I can't.

JOAN. Try.

COHN. I tried once. Look what happened!

JOAN. It came true.

COHN. It didn't come true. Certain things happened— I can't go into details—you don't know everything—

JOAN. You refuse to wish.

COHN. Let's drop the subject.

JOAN. You don't want it to come true.

COHN. I said—

JOAN. You don't want your friend back.

COHN. I want quiet! I want peace and quiet!

JOAN. But not your friend.

COHN. Him too! But first, quiet!

JOAN. Then wish!

COHN. You're a child!

JOAN. Wish!

COHN. Games!

JOAN. Wish!

COHN. Nag! Shrew! I wish! All right? I wish!

JOAN. What?

COHN. I wish Abe was back! (*Light and music effect.*) You satisfied? So where is he? You see him? Where is he? (JOAN *looks around.*) You're so smart. (*She looks in the bedroom.*) Miss know-it-all. (*He turns his back on her in contempt. She comes out of the bedroom, opens the lid of the trunk and looks in.*)

JOAN. It came true!

COHN. (*He whirls, looks on in horror.*) Close it! What are you doing in there? Mind your own business!

JOAN. Come! Look!

COHN. Who do you think you are!

JOAN. Dear God! He's dead! (*Crosses herself.* COHN *retreats.*) Your friend is dead.

COHN. He's not dead.

JOAN. He is dead.

COHN. *He's* dead. But Abe's not dead.

JOAN. But this is Abe.

COHN. He's not Abe. Abe is alive.

JOAN. You poor man. Your mind has cracked in grief. This is Abe.

COHN. Abe is shorter.

JOAN. This man is short.

COHN. Abe doesn't have a beard.

JOAN. This man is clean-shaven.

COHN. Abe is swarthy.

JOAN. In life this man was swarthy.

COHN. (*Crosses over to the trunk, fed up.*) For once and for all— (*Looks in trunk.*) Abe! (*Falls into the*

trunk in a dead faint, head first. JOAN *rushes to trunk,*
pulls COHN *out by his shoulders and tries to lift him*
off his knees.) Go away. Leave me alone. (*Drops head*
first back into trunk. JOAN *pulls him out again . . .*
COHN *rises shakily, staggering on the run behind his*
curtained doorway. After the briefest of pauses JOAN
follows.)

JOAN. I know what's on your mind.

COHN. Go. The Emperor's waiting. *Give it back!*
(*His shotgun comes flying out through the curtain,*
lands on floor beyond trunk.)

JOAN. Did I hurt you?

COHN. Go, please go.

JOAN. What if *I* brought him back to life?

COHN. Lady—

JOAN. Would you then go with me to see the Emperor?

COHN. Oy!

JOAN. If I brought Abe back to life?

COHN. If you brought Abe back to life I'd believe
you were Jesus Christ himself. Don't hit me!

JOAN. Don't blaspheme!

COHN. Don't nag!

JOAN. Would you believe?

COHN. Would I believe? I'd believe! I'd believe!
(ABE's *legs twitch.*)

JOAN. That I am Joan?

COHN. All right!

JOAN. And you will follow me?

COHN. All right!

(ABE's *legs twitch again. His head appears out of the*
trunk. He climbs out, looks at his typewriter,
punches a key, and crosses to the refrigerator.)

ABE. Cohn! What's to eat? (COHN *appears in the*
doorway. He cannot believe his eyes. He starts to col-
lapse. JOAN *catches him and helps him to a chair.* ABE

*turns around and sees them. He shuts the refrigerator
door and stares coldly at* JOAN.) Company?

COHN. You're dead.

ABE. (*Coldly.*) I didn't know you were having a
party.

COHN. You're walking—you're talking— (*He rises,
starts to* ABE.)

ABE. I hope I'm not getting in the way. I know no
body invited me. I just live here.

COHN. (*Goes to* ABE *and embraces him.*) He lives,
he breathes— (*Holds* ABE *away from him and stares
at him happily.*) He smells!

ABE. You're drunk.

COHN. (*To* JOAN.) Has there ever been such a
friend, to rise from the dead in a rotten mood? I love
this man! (*Hugs* ABE. ABE *breaks free.*)

ABE. I beg your pardon. That person?

COHN. That's Joan! Joan, here's Abe!

ABE. I beg your pardon. An old friend?

COHN. How old is old? Ten minutes? A half hour?
It feels like half a lifetime. It was *your* lifetime, that
I'll tell you!

ABE. Riddles. You invited her?

COHN. Not two minutes ago you were dead.

ABE. You wish.

COHN. I wished you back. They sent you back dead.

ABE. Intrigue is going on here. This is my house. I
beg your pardon, Miss. It's not personal. The house is
in my name. But can I ever invite guests? Who was
my last guest? Fifteen years ago. I'll show you the
guest book. Look—here's the guest book. Blank, see?
Hundreds of pages—wait, here's the guest—no, it re-
minds me—not even a real guest—a Jehovah's Witness. Came in out of the blue. We had coffee, a pleasant
chat about religion. Cohn, here, throws a fit. Facts are
facts, Cohn. It's nothing personal, Miss. Cohn and I
don't entertain. He agreed and I agreed. When we
entertain we differ. It ends up in a fight. So we agreed

to live and let live and not entertain. I didn't make up the rule. Now he breaks it. Is this a way to run a household? Anarchy?! I beg your pardon, Cohn, I thought we'd agreed—anarchy is for outside.

COHN. (*To* JOAN.) Is that a mouth? I love that mouth! (*Beaming at him.*) Abe, not five minutes ago you know what you were?

ABE. What?

COHN. You weren't! That's what you were. You were *not!* You were dead! You were dead! You were dead! (*Smile slowly fades.*) You weren't dead. (*Turns to* JOAN.) He wasn't dead.

JOAN. He was dead.

COHN. How could he be alive if he was dead?

JOAN. You saw him!

COHN. For half a second.

JOAN. He was cold.

COHN. Who felt him?

JOAN. I did!

COHN. I thought you were a Saint. Now you're a doctor?

JOAN. You're reneging on your promise.

COHN. Don't be foolish; he only fainted.

ABE. I didn't faint.

COHN. You fainted.

ABE. Never!

COHN. In the trunk.

ABE. In what trunk?

COHN. That trunk!

ABE. I never fainted in a trunk in my life.

COHN. Not five minutes ago!

ABE. Five minutes ago I was sitting in my chair like always.

COHN. Then how come you didn't see her come in? (ABE *is stopped.*) Because you fainted!

ABE. Because you sneaked her in here before! When I wasn't looking!

COHN. *What* before?

ABE. Who knows, with a man as corrupt as you?! It could have been *years!* Who is she? Why is she wearing that armor?!

COHN. You're all excited. Calm down.

ABE. I don't like betrayal. I beg your pardon.

COHN. There's no betrayal.

ABE. Consorting with the outside.

COHN. No—

ABE. Spreading false rumors.

COHN. Abe, listen—calm now—what's the very last thing you remember?

ABE. Your betrayal.

COHN. (*Reasonably.*) Abe, *I* fainted and *I* remember.

ABE. I never fainted in my life! I beg your pardon, but I have never vomited, I have never fainted and I have never gotten drunk. Certain things I do not do. I have never done. So you and your chippie, don't try to pull a fast one.

COHN. (*Stares hard at him.*) You were dead. (*To* JOAN.) It's the only explanation. He was dead.

ABE. I didn't faint so I must be dead. That's logic.

COHN. Not now, before.

ABE. How could I be dead before and alive now? That's consistency.

COHN. Wait a minute! Stop the presses! Is this my old friend Abe talking? The very Abe who believes in genies and three wishes and that I could be Mozart and him Jefferson?

ABE. There's no inconsistency.

COHN. No inconsistency?!

ABE. It's perfectly plausible that I could die Abe and come back somebody else, but is it plausible that I should die Abe and come back Abe?

COHN. Is it plausible that you should die *Jefferson* and come back Abe?

ABE. —in the same house, with the same Cohn? A frog into a Prince I could believe. Change! That's plausible! But sameness! Eternal sameness! No, I beg your pardon, I can't be convinced.

COHN. (*Exasperated.*) I'm through wasting my breath.

(JOAN *crosses to* ABE. *He backs away. She takes his hand and stares into his eyes.*)

JOAN. I am Joan of Arc.

ABE. It's possible. You could be anybody. I won't fight over it.

COHN. He doesn't believe you.

ABE. It doesn't matter what I believe, it's what you believe.

COHN. She believes you were dead!

ABE. (*To* COHN.) That's her privilege.

JOAN. You *were* dead.

ABE. (*To* JOAN.) As far as you were concerned. You never saw me, I never saw you. In that sense I was dead.

JOAN. I brought you back to life.

ABE. In a physical way? Well, who knows? It's been a long time. But I do feel a certain arousal—

COHN. (*Groans and buries his head in his hands.*) It's not opinion! It's not an argument. It's a fact. A fact! A fact! She's Joan of Arc! She has voices! She brought you back to life! (*To* JOAN.) Strike him dead and bring him back again! (*To* ABE.) And this time pay attention!

ABE. You ask me is this Abe? I ask you is this Cohn? You believe she's Joan of Arc?

COHN. No doubt about it.

ABE. And I was dead?

COHN. No question.

ABE. And she brought me back to life?

COHN. Believe me, it's a mixed blessing.

ABE. (*To* JOAN.) Huh—must you be able to argue!

COHN. I believe in what's concrete—in what I see,

until I see something different. That at least is consistent. (*To* JOAN.) Are you ready?

JOAN. You'll come with me to see the Emperor?

ABE. Now comes an Emperor.

COHN. She and I have a mission!

JOAN. (*To* ABE.) And you too.

ABE. Me? I'm dead.

JOAN. You won't come with us?

ABE. I beg your pardon. Two's company, three's a crowd.

COHN. Look, are we going to go or are we going to stay here and argue?

ABE. I don't want to keep you.

JOAN. (*Confused.*) I'm not sure I should leave you.

COHN. Joan—any time you're ready.

ABE. Twenty years, Cohn, and now you go outside.

COHN. I'm not rigid!

ABE. You've changed!

COHN. Is that a crime?

ABE. (*Deeply disturbed.*) It's—it's a miracle! (*To* JOAN.) To change Cohn—to make him move an inch, not to mention he goes outside is nothing less than a miracle. Who are you?

JOAN. I told you.

ABE. (*Stares at her for a long time.*) It's possible.

JOAN. Then you'll come?

ABE. Impossible.

JOAN. You have to come!

COHN. You can't stay here alone.

ABE. I'll manage.

COHN. Who'll cook for you?

ABE. I'll learn.

COHN. You won't learn.

ABE. Then I won't learn.

COHN. You'll starve.

ABE. It's possible. But unlikely.

COHN. (*To* JOAN.) I don't have all day, you know.

JOAN. We must go. (*Opens front door.* COHN *goes out.*)

COHN. Hey, it's not so bad! (JOAN *takes a long, sad look at* ABE.)

FIRST VOICE. Joan—

JOAN. (*Freezes.*) Yes.

ABE. What's that?

SECOND VOICE. You can't leave.

ABE. Who said that?

JOAN. But my mission—

FIRST VOICE. Your mission is to take two of every kind.

ABE. (*Looks around.*) Who said that?

JOAN. I know.

FIRST VOICE. That includes schleppes.

ABE. (*Still looking.*) Who said that?

FIRST VOICE. You need one more.

(ABE *walks around looking for the Voices.* JOAN *moves away from the door, back into the room.* COHN *appears in the doorway.*)

COHN. Well? (*Nobody moves.*)

CURTAIN

ACT TWO

*A Month Later. The house is no less cramped but
much more orderly, like a military barracks. The
screen has been moved from the kitchen to a
corner near the bedrooms where it partially hides
a sloppily made army cot in which* COHN *presently
sleeps. Lying across the foot of the cot is a violin,
several cookbooks and the Bible.* COHN *sits in his
chair at the oak table. His head is bowed, his
hands clasped, praying.* ABE *comes out of his bedroom, obviously ill at ease in* COHN's *presence.
He crosses to the typewriter, stares at the nearly
blank sheet and punches a key.* COHN *looks up.*
ABE, *refusing to meet his eyes, turns and disappears into his room.* COHN *looks heavenward.*

COHN. God? Cohn again. How long? That's all I
ask. The main thing is the waiting. How important in
the scheme of things, one Abe more or less. The suffering I don't mind. In fact, so far it's minimal, to be
frank, non-existent, to tell you the truth, a pleasure.
But if I had to, believe me, suffering! Sacrifice! You
say the word, it's a commitment. For that girl—*and
you*—it's you name it! (JOAN *enters from* COHN's
bedroom. COHN *jumps up in embarrassment.*) Speak
of the devil!

JOAN. How proud of you I am, Cohn.

COHN. You're proud, I'm proud, we're both proud.
You changed my life.

JOAN. Not I. God.

COHN. You first. You gave me proof. Tangibles.

JOAN. Faith is the absence of proof.

COHN. Still it needs a beginning.

JOAN. From within!

COHN. You want something to eat? I have on a veal loaf. It'll be ready in no time. First start with this. (*Hands her a plate of antipasto.*)

JOAN. I shouldn't, really. It's delicious.

COHN. Eat. (*Watches her eat.*) You take small bites for a soldier.

JOAN. I can't help but think of all those who go hungry.

COHN. Soon that will end. (JOAN *plows into her food.*) It *will* end soon, won't it?

JOAN. (*Eating compulsively.*) What?

COHN. Hunger. Famine.

JOAN. When?

COHN. When?!

JOAN. (*In mid-bite.*) Oh, heaven! You mean heaven! Of course! (*Resumes eating.*) I'm sorry, this is so delicious that I— (*Puts plate down.*)

COHN. No. Finish. Finish.

JOAN. (*Hesitates.*) God's will be done. I am his servant. (*Resumes eating passionately.*)

(*A warm exchange of stares.* ABE *enters, sees* COHN *and* JOAN *together, starts to back-pedal to his room.* JOAN *spots him and rises.*)

ABE. I beg your pardon. (*Crosses to stove as if crossing a mine field.*) I'll be out of your way in a minute. (*Pours himself a cup of coffee. With sudden resentment.*) Far be it for me to make a pest of myself.

JOAN. (*Starts toward him.*) Abe—

ABE. (*Circles around her.*) Abe's my name. Invisibility's my game. (*Disappears behind his curtain.*)

JOAN. He won't let me talk to him.

COHN. That's his problem.

JOAN. *Our* problem! (ABE, *his collar raised so as to make him invisible, slinks out again.*)

ABE. I'm not even here. (ABE *crosses to the refriger-*

*ator and takes out a container of milk. On his way
back* JOAN *plants herself in his path.* ABE *stops, turns
and starts back to the refrigerator. He opens it and
sticks his head in as far as it will go, pretending to
look for something.* JOAN *comes up behind him and
stands there.* ABE *retreats even further into the refrigerator, until more of him is in than out.)*

JOAN. May I say something, Abe? (*A long wait.*)
I'd like to speak to you. (JOAN *does not move.* ABE
does not move. Finally he sneezes. Instinctively JOAN
puts a hand on his shoulder.) Abe—

(ABE *reacts as if he's been shot. His head jerks up
against the roof of the fridge with a resounding
clunk. Stunned, his entire body, or what we see
of it, sags. If we can see his head, it now lies on
the first shelf.* JOAN *drags him out, closes the door
and half carries him to his chair.*)

ABE. I never felt better.
JOAN. Abe, why don't you speak to me? (ABE *doesn't
answer.*) I've been here for weeks and we haven't ex-
changed a dozen words.
ABE. A dozen eggs?
JOAN. A dozen words.
ABE. What do you want to exchange a dozen words
for? Are they dirty? How do I know you even bought
them here?
JOAN. You confuse me, Abe.
ABE. Confusme. That's a Chinese philosopher.
JOAN. That's Confucius.
ABE. Confucius is a color.
JOAN. That's fuchsia.
ABE. Fuchsia is what you say when there's a bad
smell.
JOAN. That's phew.
ABE. Phew is a body of water in Norway.
JOAN. That's fjord.

ABE. Fjord is a car.

JOAN. That's Ford.

ABE. Ford is the number after three.

JOAN. That's four.

ABE. What's four?

JOAN. A number!

ABE. Absolutely right, I was so cold I was number. (*Rises.*) It's a pleasure finally talking to you. (*He staggers on the run into his room.* JOAN *looks after him, then turns to* COHN *who, all this while has been glaring sullenly at the scene. He turns away from her.* JOAN *crosses to him.*)

JOAN. Tell me what to do, Cohn.

COHN. (*Brusque.*) Forget it.

JOAN. (*Squeezes his shoulder.*) God depends on you, Cohn.

COHN. God? (*He rises, very haughtily.*) Sometimes, very frankly, it's hard to take some of this stuff seriously. (COHN *walks past her into the kitchen and busies himself at the stove.* JOAN *crosses to darkened window, looks out.*)

JOAN. (*Softly.*) Voices? I see signs. I think it's going well. (*Looks around with some anxiety.*) Voices!?

FIRST VOICE. What now?

SECOND VOICE. Yes, Joan.

JOAN. I'm really very encouraged.

FIRST VOICE. She's encouraged.

SECOND VOICE. It doesn't take much.

JOAN. I have faith! They are almost ready.

SECOND VOICE. Joan—

FIRST VOICE. What are we going to do with her?

JOAN. I don't understand. Don't you think things are going well? Cohn is with me, that's one . . .

SECOND VOICE. I'll say he's one.

JOAN. And now that Abe is talking to me—

SECOND VOICE. Joan, come to your senses.

JOAN. Didn't you see it? *He is talking to me!*

SECOND VOICE. Talk to her.

FIRST VOICE. You talk to her.

SECOND VOICE. Who can talk to her? You talk to her.

FIRST VOICE. I don't want to talk to her. Frankly, I'm heartsick.

JOAN. What in the world is wrong with you today, Voices?

SECOND VOICE. Will you listen to the mouth on her?

FIRST VOICE. (*Warning.*) Take it back, Joan!

JOAN. (*Fearful.*) I'm unworthy! I take it back! (*Pause. Confused.*) What?

FIRST VOICE. She doesn't know.

SECOND VOICE. Hopeless.

JOAN. What? Am I displeasing you? I thought everything was wonderful. (*Grabs for her plate, eats compulsively.*)

SECOND VOICE. Stuffs herself like a pig.

FIRST VOICE. Any second now—crash!—armor all over the place.

JOAN. Why are you so angry with me? (*Hesitates in her eating. Reluctantly puts down plate.*) I am the servant of the Lord. I do his bidding.

FIRST VOICE. Will you look at her complexion? Breaking out.

SECOND VOICE. And why not? She hasn't been out of the house in a month.

FIRST VOICE. I think that you are losing your faith, Joan.

JOAN. Never!

SECOND VOICE. Not five minutes ago you forgot about heaven.

JOAN. Not for a second!

FIRST VOICE. Admit it! When you were eating.

JOAN. It slipped my mind for one second. Is that a mortal sin?

SECOND VOICE. Are you questioning us?

JOAN. I'm asking—

SECOND VOICE. Questioning!

JOAN. Not seriously—
SECOND VOICE. Losing faith.
JOAN. I have faith!
SECOND VOICE. Faith to do what?
JOAN. To believe!
SECOND VOICE. Believe in what?
JOAN. Believe in my Voices!
FIRST VOICE. We don't want you to say it if you don't mean it.
JOAN. With all my heart and soul! Before my Voices what was I? But with my Voices who am I? Do you think I can overlook such change? But it's so hard. Cohn, no matter what I say, he will agree. But to what end? No end. And Abe hates me. I know he hates me. Why shoud he hate me?
FIRST VOICE. Nobody said it would be easy.
SECOND VOICE. You must strengthen your faith. Strong faith sweeps all before it.
FIRST VOICE. Faith can move mountains, Joan.
JOAN. Voices! Let me go to a mountain!
SECOND VOICE. Joan, your trial is here.
JOAN. I beg of you, let me first move a mountain.
FIRST VOICE. Can you believe this?
JOAN. I promise, Voices, I shall make good on a mountain, then I shall return here.
FIRST VOICE. Hopeless!
SECOND VOICE. Admit it, we picked a real lemon this time.

(JOAN *whirls as a rock crashes through the window and lands at her feet.* COHN *and* ABE *come running. All stare down at the rock.* JOAN *stoops to pick it up.*)

COHN. Don't touch!
ABE. It's an animal!
COHN. It's a bomb!
ABE. It's not a bomb.

COHN. It's not an animal. (JOAN *reaches for it.*)

ABE and COHN. Don't pick it up! (JOAN *picks it up.*)

JOAN. It's a rock.

COHN. Get it away! Away! I hear ticking!

ABE. There's writing on it.

COHN. Who writes on rocks?

ABE. Who writes on bombs?

COHN. (*A wave of dismissal.*) Later!

JOAN. It's a message!

COHN. Don't read it!

ABE. Who writes on rocks? It says—

JOAN. (*Reading.*) "You will meet new challenges which can be turned into opportunities. Beware of January, February and March."

COHN. (*Crosses to window. Shouts.*) Get away from here! This is no time for jokes!

(*A knock on the door. All jump. JOAN goes to the door. An aged, stooped MESSENGER in a cap. [WISEMAN].*)

MESSENGER. I have a rock for Joan of Arc.

JOAN. I'll take it.

MESSENGER. You Joan of Arc? (JOAN *nods.*) Sign here, please. (JOAN *signs his pad. He hands her the rock, then stares at her.*) You really Joan of Arc?

JOAN. I am.

MESSENGER. (*Begins to chuckle and shake his head.*) Joan of Arc. (JOAN *gently closes the door on the chuckling* MESSENGER. *She reads the rock.*)

JOAN. "Beware of April, May and June." (*With a loud squeal, the refrigerator door swings open.* JOAN, COHN, *and* ABE *look up. A rock falls out of the refrigerator.* JOAN *drops the second rock and crosses to the new rock. She kneels and reads it.*) "Also July, August, September, October, November, December."

ABE. That's it as far as I'm concerned. (*He crosses on the run into his bedroom.* COHN *crosses to the door.*)

COHN. (*Whispers.*) While it's still dark let's make a break.

JOAN. Not without Abe.

COHN. (*Fed up.*) Abe?! Who knows what's out there?

JOAN. And I believed you had faith.

COHN. (*Conspiritorial.*) You want Abe? (*Takes drug off stock shelf.*) A pinch of this in Abe's soup. In no time, out like a baby. I guarantee after twenty years inside, we get him outside, he won't leave our side.

JOAN. (*Disbelieving.*) You want me to trick Abe?

COHN. Tactics. You never heard of tactics? All right, you don't like pharmacology, here's plan two. While he was inside hiding, he missed a second messenger. A Hollywood offer. Big money. A documentary. A movie pilgrimage to the Emperor. Trust me, if Abe falls for it, we can handle the others.

JOAN. (*Puzzled.*) You want me to fool Abe?

COHN. Who wouldn't want to be in pictures? They'll fall for it, two of every kind. I guarantee: a cast of thousands.

JOAN. (*Shocked.*) You want me to lie?

COHN. First and last we remember the mission. Later is time enough for the truth.

JOAN. From the beginning!

COHN. The beginning's too soon for unorganized truth. It needs preparation. You don't like movies? Here's plan three. We'll say we're the police, charges have been made but it's a free country. They'll have their day in court, they should come with us to appeal before the Emperor.

JOAN. Cohn, what's come over you?

COHN. You give them a little fear, they get a move on. No dillydally. No explanations. The main thing is the mission.

JOAN. You actually want me to lie!

COHN. It's no bed of roses out there. In me, you're fortunate to find a man of imagination, but out there, you tell them you're Joan of Arc, I guarantee it's no laugh riot.

JOAN. They will believe me.

COHN. *What?* Two bricklayers? Two carpenters? Two truckdrivers? Two taxi drivers? Two advertising agency executives? Joan. Joan, what am I going to do with you? It's a whirlpool you're walking into. Not even you can walk on whirlpools. It takes fiddling. A story here. A little piece of business there. You maneuver. You manipulate. Push comes to shove, a wheel, a deal, we got ourselves an army. Trust me.

JOAN. I trust God.

COHN. No argument. No argument. He gives policy, I carry it out. Where's the contradiction?

JOAN. I trust my voices.

COHN. Voices always have to be right? Believe me, Joan, I've worked this out.

JOAN. Believe you? I can scarcely believe my senses!

COHN. Voices talk, they don't listen. They're Voices. What do they know? Two of every kind. Abe and me? Never! Not in a million years! Even superficially— Glutton. Gourmet. If they could see they'd know.

JOAN. They do know.

COHN. I can make a mistake, you can make a mistake. Voices can't make mistakes? That's not in the realm of possibility?

JOAN. How can you have faith and still question?

COHN. I don't question.

JOAN. Cohn, has questioning ever given you satisfaction?

COHN. The opposite. I don't question.

JOAN. Has it ever made you happy?

COHN. Not once. I don't question.

JOAN. Do you believe I am Joan?

COHN. Yes.

JOAN. Do you believe in my mission?

COHN. *Yes!*

JOAN. Do you believe the sky is missing?

COHN. Yes! Yes! Yes!

JOAN. Praise the Lord!

COHN. Praise the Lord!

JOAN. (*Takes his hand.*) You are my right hand, Cohn.

COHN. (*Falls to his knees, clasps her hands.*) You want to know who's two of the same kind, not Abe and me, *you* and me! More than that is a complication. Do we need it? In my opinion: no. Travel fast, travel light. We go it alone! Trust me! (*He strides to the door and throws it open.*)

(*A* SOLDIER *in combat dress, wearing a gas mask and carrying an automatic rifle, stands in the doorway.* COHN, *still staring at* JOAN, *does not see him. He holds his hand out, beckoning her to the great outdoors. His hand brushes against the* SOLDIER'S *gas mask. He turns, very slowly, to see what he's touching, sees, and slams shut the door. A siren sounds. The room is flooded with searchlights.*)

POLICE VOICE. (WISEMAN—*Miked.*) Send out the girl! We only want the girl!

ABE. (*Crawling out of his room on his belly.*) I knew it!

POLICE VOICE. We don't want you. We only want the girl.

COHN. (*Shouts.*) There's no girl here!

ABE. (*Whispers.*) Don't make trouble!

JOAN. I'll go!

COHN. (*Stops her.*) No!

POLICE VOICE. We don't want you, we only want the girl.

ABE. (*Shouts.*) You can have her! You can have her!

COHN. (*To* ABE.) *You* go!

ABE. Ah hah! Didn't I know it?!

COHN. You're so smart, you go!

POLICE VOICE. We don't want Abe, we want the girl.

JOAN. Let me speak to them!

COHN. They're your enemies.

JOAN. I have no enemies.

ABE. She has no enemies, let her go.

COHN. (*Restraining* JOAN.) No! *I'll* go!

POLICE VOICE. We don't want Cohn, we want the girl.

COHN. (*Shouts.*) It's all or nothing!

ABE. All? What all?!

COHN. You want her, you got to kill us all!

ABE. Kill us all?!

POLICE VOICE. We don't want to kill you all, we only want to kill the girl.

COHN. (*To* JOAN.) See?

JOAN. They won't harm me. They are my army!

COHN. Are you crazy? You're Joan of Arc! They want to burn you at the stake!

POLICE VOICE. There'll be a hot time in the old town tonight!

JOAN. Voices!

POLICE VOICE. Yes?

JOAN. I want *my* Voices!

POLICE VOICE. The game's up, sister. Throw out your armor and come out with your hands up!

JOAN. He's drowning out my Voices!

POLICE VOICE. (*Croons.*)

I dream of Joannie with the light blonde hair . . .

(*As* POLICE VOICE *sings* ABE *leaps into the trunk and pulls the lid down over him.* COHN *dashes for the bedroom and comes out with his shotgun.* JOAN, *at the door, tries to pull it open. It is locked, she fiddles with the bolt. By this time,* COHN *is at the window and fires a blast.*) Very nice! (*A white flag is poked through the shattered window.*) Don't shoot. I'm coming in to parley.

(*The door opens.* JOAN *leaps back. In walks* WISEMAN,

in robes as before, but with a gold star pinned to his chest. He crosses to the table, sits, puts on a green eyeshade and begins shuffling a deck of cards. COHN backs off in horror.)

WISEMAN. To make it interesting we play for the girl. *(Looks at them.)* Who plays? *(Stares at COHN who backs into the trunk. ABE lifts the lid and peers out at WISEMAN. He climbs out of the trunk as COHN climbs in and pulls shut the lid. ABE crosses to WISEMAN and sits.)*

ABE. We play for peace and quiet.

WISEMAN. I win I get the girl, you win you get peace and quiet. *(He deals the cards. They study their hands. As each discards, he calls out his card.)* 55.

ABE. 71.

WISEMAN. King.

ABE. Einstein.

WISEMAN. Queen.

ABE. Garbo.

WISEMAN. Jack.

ABE. Daniels.

WISEMAN. One.

ABE. Meatball.

WISEMAN. Ashtray.

ABE. Match.

WISEMAN. Deuce.

ABE. Game.

WISEMAN. Loophole.

ABE. Manhole.

WISEMAN. Fix.

ABE. Parking ticket.

WISEMAN. Horse.

ABE. Fire engine.

WISEMAN. Love.

ABE. Stock market.

WISEMAN. Cadillac.

ABE. Morphine.

WISEMAN. Mortuary.

ABE. February.

WISEMAN. Wake.

ABE. Corn flakes.

WISEMAN. Banco!

ABE. Bunko!

WISEMAN. (*Fans out his cards.*) An inside straight!

ABE. (*Fans out his cards.*) An outside patio with a rose garden! (WISEMAN *growls, kicks over his chair and storms out.*)

JOAN. (*Crosses to* ABE.) You are a wonderful card player. (ABE *doesn't look at her. He shuffles the cards.* JOAN *sits next to him.* ABE *continues to shuffle.*)

ABE. I'll give you the answer, you give me the question, Chicken teriyaki.

JOAN. I don't understand.

ABE. I'll give you the answer. You give me the question. It's a game.

JOAN. Oh.

ABE. Chicken teriyaki. (JOAN *looks at him nonplussed.*) You don't know? The question is: Who is the oldest living kamikaze pilot? Here's another: 9–W. (JOAN *doesn't respond.*) Now you give me the question.

JOAN. I wasn't listening.

ABE. The answer is 9–W. What's the question?

JOAN. I don't know.

ABE. The question is: Do you spell your name with a "V," Herr Wagner? You ready for another?

JOAN. (*She reaches out to him.*) Abe—

ABE. (*He pulls away. A pause.*) All right, here's another. The answer is: From birth, I was taught to believe: Where there's a will, there's a way. But nobody wrote me into his will, so I had to make my own way. Still, I had hope. Some day I would find the right situation. In the meantime I piled up money. For when I found the right situation. Also I married. A mistake, but bearable. It didn't take too much of either of our time. Whenever we exchanged understanding stares,

I found out later it was a misunderstanding. So I wondered: Is this all? I couldn't accept yes for an answer, so I left my wife and I started looking. She sent Cohn to bring me back. Instead, he talked me into looking where he wanted to look instead of where I wanted. Finally, we split up. I went on looking. High and low, inside and out, until I got so depressed I couldn't hold my head up. So not being able to hold my head up I saw straight in front of me for the first time. And looking right in my face was the answer. In life you don't look too high and you don't look too low, you look straight down the middle. The answer lies in the middle. In the middle there's always room for hope and not too much room for disappointment. So the lesson of life is to settle. So I came to the woods. To settle. I found this house, I knocked on the door and Cohn opened it. He had settled the year before me. It's not terrific. But also it's not painful. I don't hurt anybody. It's an across the board settlement. I don't love it, I don't hate it. That's the answer, what's the question?

JOAN. The question is: If you want to believe in something, can't you come up with anything better than that? (*They continue to stare at each other.*)

ABE. I beg your pardon. (*Rises, looks at typewriter, punches a key, looks at paper, pulls it out and crumples it.*) I'll put it this way. I'll start. How far I get is another question.

JOAN. (*Slowly realizing.*) You'll go? You'll come?

ABE. (*Smiles.*) I'll accompany. (*Backs off into his doorway where he lingers for a moment, then disappears.*)

JOAN. You'll accompany! You'll accompany! Cohn! (*Looks for him.*) Abe will accompany! (COHN *lifts the lid of the trunk an inch or two and peers out.*) Abe will accompany! He'll accompany!

ABE. (*Pokes his head out from behind his curtain.*) Miss? Joan? Could you possibly— (JOAN *charges through* ABE'S *curtain.* COHN *stands up in the trunk and looks after her.*)

COHN. He'll change his mind! I know him!

JOAN. (*Pokes her head out from behind curtain.*) He's beginning to pack! (*Ducks back in.*)

COHN. It's a lie! He's lying!

JOAN. (*Pokes her head out.*) He's packing! He's actually packing! (*Ducks back in.*)

COHN. I've been through this before!

JOAN. (*Pokes her head out.*) Do you know where he put his muffler? He won't go outside without his muffler! (*Back in.*)

COHN. He's backing down!

JOAN. (*Head out.*) He found his muffler! (*Back in.*)

COHN. It's the wrong muffler!

JOAN. (*Head out.*) He's packed! (*Back in.*)

COHN. He's not to be trusted!

JOAN. (*Head out.*) He's putting on his galoshes! (*Back in.*)

COHN. We can't wait! He'll slow us down!

JOAN. (*Head out.*) He's coming!

COHN. We'll never get there!

JOAN. (*Throws open curtain and introduces* ABE.) He's *here!* (ABE *emerges past* JOAN, *bandaged in winter clothes, lugging a huge suitcase.*)

ABE. What a sensational day for a trip!

JOAN. Onward to the Emperor!

SECOND VOICE. Onward to the Emperor!

(ABE *and* JOAN *move to the door.* JOAN *throws open the door.* COHN *disappears into the trunk and slams shut the lid.* ABE *and* JOAN *stand watching.*)

COHN. (*Raises the lid one-half inch.*) You know what you can do with those buttinsky, wiseacre voices of yours? I *wish* you never heard of them! You know what I *wish*—I *wish* you never heard of Joan of Arc! (*Slams shut the lid. Light and music effect.*)

JOAN. (*Puts on bandanna cap, grabs broom, starts sweeping. Turns to* ABE.) Abe, what are you all bundled up for? (*Starts unwrapping him.*) You're not going out in this weather. After dark? In the night air? Without your dinner? Cohn, can you imagine? Honestly! You two! What am I ever going to do with you? (*She continues to unbundle the stunned* ABE. COHN *stands up in the trunk and looks on.*)

CURTAIN

ACT THREE

*Five months later. The house is as cramped as before
and far more disorganized. Everything looks as
if it's been moved and for no particular purpose.
Altogether the impression is of impeding chaos.
JOAN'S tarnished armor hangs in sections on several hooks of a clothes tree. It is dinner time. Two
pots on the stove give off lots of steam. The dining room table is littered with dirty dishes. ABE'S
typewriter and stacks of paper are nowhere in
sight. ABE comes out from behind his curtained
doorway wearing a bathrobe, carrying a half
empty glass of milk. He brushes past JOAN'S
armor.*

ABE. In the way. As usual. (*He stops, scowls at the
armor, then tentatively touches it. He takes the head-
piece off its hook, is about to try it on when JOAN
rises out of the steam from behind the kitchen counter.
She wears an old-fashioned flowered dress and a frilly
apron. Her complexion is pale and waxen.*)

JOAN. (*Excited.*) Almost ready! (*She lifts the cover
off a pot, burns her hand on the handle, and lets go
with a loud scream. The cover flies across the room
through COHN'S curtained doorway. COHN rushes out,
holding pot cover. He is a smoother looking, less
abrasive COHN.*)

COHN. Joan—

JOAN. (*Whirls on him.*) Stay put!

COHN. (*Freezes.*) But—

JOAN. If it didn't belong there I wouldn't have
thrown it there! (*Turns back to stove.*) One more
minute!

COHN. (*Not daring to move.*) It smells delicious!

ABE. (*Crosses to table and sits.*) It was one more minute fifteen minutes ago.

JOAN. Cooking one thing at a time is no problem, it's cooking combinations.

ABE. If excuses were only edible.

COHN. (*To* ABE.) She's trying.

ABE. If reasons were raisins I wouldn't go hungry.

JOAN. (*Whirls on* ABE.) What did you say?

ABE. Me? Not a word.

JOAN. (*Turns back to stove.*) The trick is to get the roast and the beans and the cauliflower and the potatoes all done at the same— I think it's ready. (*Opens the oven door. Thick black smoke spurts out, darkening* JOAN's *face and sending her into a fit of coughing. She grabs a dish towel and covers her face. Staggering around, she backs into the stove and knocks the pots off.*)

COHN. (*Alarmed.*) Careful!

JOAN *manages to escape the downpour of boiling water and vegetables. In her jumping about she sends the spice shelf flying. In her attempt to regain her balance she flails out and grabs hold of the bottom shelf of the dish cabinet. The shelf gives way and all the dishes descend on her.* JOAN *disappears from view under a pile of debris.* COHN *leans forward tensely,* ABE *leans back, contemptuous.*)

ABE. Typical. (COHN *starts toward the kitchen.*)

JOAN. (*Out of sight.*) Everyone stay out of here. (COHN *keeps coming. He gets to the kitchen.* JOAN *screams.*) Stay out! I had a little accident. No one's hurt. (*Snarls to* COHN.) Everything's under control.

COHN. (*Advances a step.*) Let me—

JOAN. (*Screams.*) *I don't need help!* (*Rises from the floor, her hair in disarray, her blouse ripped, but with a blackened roast pig on a platter, an apple in its mouth. She marches proudly to the dining table and slams down the platter.*) No vegetables tonight. (*Glares at* COHN.) All right?

COHN. Fine.

JOAN. (*Glares at* ABE.) All right?

ABE. I had vegetables yesterday.

(COHN *starts carving the pig.* JOAN *goes back to the kitchen and begins sweeping up the wreckage. It makes a terrific clatter.*)

COHN. Don't you want to eat, Joan?

JOAN. (*Snaps.*) Later.

COHN. Don't you at least want to sit with us?

JOAN. (*Snaps.*) Later. (COHN *sighs and starts eating.*)

ABE. A terrific companion. If she wasn't so handy around the kitchen I'd suggest we get rid of her.

COHN. (*Low.*) She hasn't been well.

ABE. (*Picks up a charred slice of pig.*) Look at that. By what stretch of the imagination could this possibly be called food?

COHN. It's not so bad.

ABE. This is a pig not even a pig would eat.

COHN. A little charity!

ABE. You want charity? Ask the Emperor!

JOAN. (*Reacts suddenly, as if in reaction to* ABE's *harsh reminder.*) Ouch!

COHN. (*Jumps up.*) What happened?

JOAN. Nothing.

COHN. You cut yourself!

JOAN. It's all right.

ABE. (*To* COHN.) Stop making a fool of yourself. Sit down.

COHN. Let me look!

JOAN. Stay put. It's only a cut finger.

COHN. Oh my God!

JOAN. (*Comes out of the kitchen, one finger aloft.*)

Oh, stop it, Cohn. Nobody dies of a cut finger. (*She faints dead away.* COHN *runs to her, scoops her up in his arms and carries her to the couch. He empties the couch of its litter and lays* JOAN *down.*)

COHN. Abe, quick! Bandages! Gauze! Iodine! Brandy! (ABE *leans back in his chair, stretches his arms and yawns.*) Heartless!

ABE. She's faking.

COHN. Heartless! Heartless!

ABE. I know a faker when I see it. You talk heaven to her, she burns a pig, talk mission, she cuts a finger, talk going outside, she falls asleep. Minnie the Moocher. Free room and board. In exchange for what? In my life among bad deals I include this with the worst.

COHN. She's dying!

ABE. She fainted. I died. And believe you me I didn't get all this attention. (COHN *rushes off for medical equipment.* ABE *strolls over to* JOAN.) All right. Have it your way for now. I'm patient. Nobody outwaits Abe. I only get fooled once. A stranger cries "Heaven!" You take a look. It's only polite, what could it hurt? If it turns out heaven, so much the better. If not, what's to lose? One more disappointment. In my life that's hardly an event. I worked on Wall Street thirty years, but for hope I was ready to take a plunge. So what do I get for my investment? People jump out the window for less. (COHN *rushes back in.* ABE *walks back to the table.*)

COHN. (*On his knees beside* JOAN.) The bleeding stopped. Look how white she is, Abe.

ABE. (*Indicates door.*) She's free to get all the air she wants. With my blessing.

COHN. You're upset, that's why you're talking that way.

ABE. Me? Do I look upset? (*He doesn't.*)

COHN. (*Eager to make up.*) I apologize for calling you heartless. It was a moment of excitement.

ABE. Who listened?

COHN. (*Confidential.*) Listen, while she's out you want me to make you a little something?

ABE. I'm not hungry.

COHN. An omelet? You love my omeletes.

ABE. I'm full. On pig.

COHN. You name it, I'll cook it.

ABE. Don't trouble yourself.

COHN. Trouble? It would be a pleasure.

ABE. Thank you, but food no longer interests me.

COHN. She's breathing more regular. (JOAN *wakes.*) Stay still.

JOAN. That's easy enough for you to say.

COHN. What's so important you can't rest a minute?

JOAN. The kitchen.

COHN. I can't clean it up?

JOAN. I don't want you in my kitchen.

COHN. I won't go near it.

JOAN. Stop humoring me.

COHN. I'm only trying to be friends.

JOAN. I have no friends.

COHN. I'm not a friend?

JOAN. You say it but you don't mean it.

COHN. I mean it with my heart.

JOAN. Abe's not my friend.

COHN. Abe is crazy about you.

JOAN. He hates me. And you're his friend so you must hate me.

COHN. Abe loves you, I love you. You're a little sick so you feel bad.

JOAN. He makes me feel useless. He's the one who's useless. If I ever get my health back, I'm going to tell him that. He's right. I am useless. I mess up everything. I don't blame him for not liking me. Sometimes I hate you.

COHN. (*Hurt, but hiding it.*) Don't worry about it.

JOAN. I bore you.

COHN. You don't!

JOAN. I bore me, so I must bore you.

COHN. The other way around.

JOAN. You mean I bore Abe too?

COHN. I mean I bore you.

JOAN. You do bore me.

COHN. (*Alarmed.*) You want to leave!

JOAN. You want me to leave.

COHN. You're bored and you want to leave.

JOAN. I don't want to leave.

COHN. Why shouldn't you?

JOAN. I'll go if you want me to.

COHN. Never!

JOAN. Where would I go?

COHN. That's all that's keeping you. If you knew where to go you'd be out of here like a shot.

JOAN. I don't want to leave.

COHN. You're saying it to make me feel good.

JOAN. What could possibly be out there that I'd want?

COHN. Nothing is out there! But if there was—

JOAN. But there isn't!

COHN. But you'd go!

JOAN. I don't care what there is—I—I wouldn't go.

COHN. I just want you to be happy.

JOAN. (*Helpless pause.*) Well, I'm mostly happy.

COHN. But you're sick.

JOAN. I'm much better.

COHN. You're weak. You take on too much. You should do less.

JOAN. If I did less I'd die.

COHN. But you're happy. (JOAN *nods.*) Well, that's all I care about. If I could believe that then I'd sleep easy.

JOAN. Aren't you sleeping well?

COHN. I worry.

JOAN. I will never go.

COHN. So I won't worry. (COHN *lays his head in her lap and starts humming a Mozart aria.* JOAN *moves* COHN's *head off her lap and stands. She takes two steps and falls into a dead faint.* COHN, *on the couch, continues humming and does not notice.* ABE *comes out of the kitchen where he's been sneaking a cold meal out of the refrigerator. He stops and looks down at* JOAN.)

ABE. (*To* JOAN.) You should be an actress on the stage. (*Stares down at her while gnawing away at a chicken leg. Suddenly he bends down to take a closer look. He feels her pulse.*) She's dying.

COHN. She's happy. (*Resumes humming.*)

ABE. (*Listens to her heart.*) She's dead. (*Rises. To* COHN.) You really did it this time. (COHN *jumps up and runs to the fallen* JOAN. ABE *walks off.*)

COHN. Water! Smelling salts! Pepper! Garlic! Brandy! (*Shakes* JOAN's *lifeless body.*) I warned her to take it easy. But no, she has to have her own way! (*Shakes her more violently.*) She won't listen! (*Strokes her face.*) Pale like a ghost. (*Flutters a hand back and forth across her face.*) She's not well enough to go out. Wake up, Joan! (*Slaps her lightly.*) Abe, where's the water? (*Looks up at* ABE *who has not moved.*) What is this? Sadism?! *Cooperate!*

ABE. It's over. You did it.

COHN. (*Shakes* JOAN, *slaps her face repeatedly.*) Wake up! (*Shakes her.*) I get no cooperation! (*Lifts her angrily and throws her on the couch.*)

ABE. Very nice.

COHN. Not one ounce of cooperation from anyone around here. It's her who's sick, not me, but does she help? Fat chance! No help! Never helps! Just faints. Faints! Faints! Faints! You could clock it on the hour. As if she has anything really wrong with her; don't tell me! Hysterical reaction. Getting even. Childish! Childish! What did I do? What was my crime! Why all this torture? If I'm a criminal, get it over, put me on trial!

(*Door flies open.* WISEMAN *enters in his robes, wearing a judge's wig and carrying law books.*)

BAILIFF'S VOICE. Oyes! Oyez! The Second Hessian of the Fourth Circuit Court of the Fifth at Aqueduct is now inoperative. Judge Helmut Wiseman presiding.

WISEMAN. (*Uprights the trunk and bangs a gavel on it.*) This court is now in session. Who represents the accursed—uh—accused?

ABE. I do, Your Honor.

WISEMAN. Who represents the prosecution?

ABE. I do, Your Honor.

COHN. So that's what you're up to! I knew it all the time! I wasn't born yesterday!

ABE. Your Honor, the defendant alleges he wasn't boring yesterday.

WISEMAN. Is he aware he's under oath?

COHN. I'm not under oath. I'm not under anything!

ABE. If Your Honor pleases, I have an expert witness who will testify that the defendant was boring yesterday.

WISEMAN. Let me admonish the defendant of the danger of committing perjury.

ABE. Your Honor, I have additional expert testimony which will prove that the defendant has been boring for twenty years; that, in fact, the defendant has a history of being boring to a point of tears, death and distraction.

WISEMAN. (*Picks up imaginary phone.*) Hello. Tears, Death and Distraction. I'm sorry, Mr. Tears is dead, Mr. Death is distracted and Mr. Distraction's in traction. I'll put you on to our Mr. Cohn. *Cohn!*

ABE. Take the stand!

WISEMAN. Do you swear to tell the truth, the whole truth, the half-truth, for better or worse, for whom the bell tolls, for me and my gal, in sickness, in health, in darkness, in light, in Newark, in Irvington, indecision, innuendo, so help you God?

COHN. Not on your life!

WISEMAN. Oh yeah?! Well, a knot on *your* life! (*Swings at* COHN's *head with the gavel.* COHN *ducks.* WISEMAN *falls off balance, over the trunk.*) Order! Did you hear me call for order?!

ABE. Fried eggs over light with bacon.

WISEMAN. Toast?

ABE. (*Raises a glass.*) To Joan of Arc.

WISEMAN. (*Stands, raises his gavel.*) To Joan of Arc.

COHN. Ah ha! I gave you enough rope, you hung yourselves. I know your game! I admit nothing.

ABE. You admit you are Cohn?

COHN. I admit I tried. Can more be asked of any man?

ABE. And you were acquainted with this Joan of Arc?

COHN. She wasn't Joan of Arc!

ABE. I object, Your Honor. Giving adverse testimony about a deceased person who is in no position to defend herself.

COHN. She fainted. She's not dead. Who knows if she even fainted? Three of the same kind! I'm the one person here who can be trusted. *You* object? *I* object!

WISEMAN. Objection sustained.

ABE. I object!

WISEMAN. Objection sustained.

ABE. Where does that leave us?

WISEMAN. I object! Objection overruled! Are there any further questions to be asked of this witness?

ABE. Cohn, do you recognize this object? (*Holds up* JOAN's *suit of armor.*)

COHN. It's a dress.

ABE. A dress. And do you recognize this object? (*Holds up* JOAN's *sword.*)

COHN. It's a broom.

ABE. A dress and a broom. Mr. Cohn— (*Raises five fingers.*) Please identify what I am now holding up.

COHN. You want to know what you're holding up?

ABE. What am I holding up?

COHN. You're holding up these proceedings. (*Turns to* WISEMAN.) Ha! (WISEMAN *bangs his gavel.*) You're all against me.

ABE. The judge is against you?

COHN. He's no judge. I know him from the old country.

ABE. I'm against you?

COHN. Tell me something I don't know.

ABE. The deceased was against you?

COHN. The worst of the lot. Look at her. I trusted her. The rest of you I knew better. You especially.

ABE. Me especially.

COHN. You especially.

ABE. Who pays for this house?

COHN. Every argument he brings it up. Move, I won't stop you.

ABE. It's my house!

COHN. I found it!

ABE. You rented. I bought!

COHN. So money makes everything all right? Is that the story? Plutocrat. Didn't I always know it? Plutocrat!

ABE. Nobody made you live with me.

COHN. I felt sorry for you. That's my weakness. Softness of heart. I took you in. I felt sorry for her, I took her in. So tell me, where's the gratitude? Him twenty years, her six months, I'm still waiting. I won't hold my breath. I'm guilty all right, guilty of being an innocent set loose in a world full of thieves. Cutthroats. Ingrates. That's my crime. Never again.

WISEMAN. The defendant has pleaded guilty of being innocent. I sentence him to hang by the neck until dead. (*To* COHN.) You want to appeal the sentence?

COHN. Drop dead.

WISEMAN. Appeal granted. Say thank you.

COHN. You could first cut my tongue out.

WISEMAN. Motion granted. (*Whips out scissors.*) Witness, do you have anything to say before I pass sentence?

COHN. No.

WISEMAN. Do you have anything to say before I pass out?

COHN. No.

WISEMAN. (*Rings a bell.*) Recess! (*Tips back in chair and falls to the floor, asleep.*)

COHN. I hope you're satisfied.

ABE. I didn't start it.

COHN. We were made fools of.

ABE. Not me.

COHN. You too.

ABE. You first!

COHN. You were of no help whatsoever!

ABE. Help *you?* You've got a mind like a closed fist. Who can argue with it? You believed that she heard voices!

COHN. I didn't!

ABE. You told me so yourself!

COHN. A metaphor!

ABE. You believed she had a mission.

COHN. No.

ABE. Yes.

COHN. Never!

ABE. Always!

COHN. Sometimes. Never always. Not even when I said it.

ABE. So why did you say it? (COHN *shrugs.*) To get back at me, that's why!

COHN. *You?*

ABE. So she'd like you better!

COHN. She *did* like me better.

ABE. Because you knew her first. Do you deny you told me she was Joan of Arc?

COHN. I don't remember. (ABE *turns away in disgust.*) A charming conceit. Did it do harm? She was cute. I liked her. She was nice—in my opinion—who knows? I wanted to please her. Pleasing a pretty girl. Is that so out of the question? I did it as a favor. A little game. A flirtation. Who understands women? I thought in time, with patience, with understanding, the power of logic, I could talk her out of it.

ABE. You *wished* her out of it.

COHN. I didn't wish! So I wished. You never wished?

ABE. You killed her!

COHN. Liar!!

ABE. You!

COHN. Killed her? Killed her? What are you saying? What a thing to say. I loved her! I believed in her! Killed her? Before her, I'd kill myself! (*Rushes over to* JOAN *and picks her up in his arms.*) The one person in this world who gave me anything! You gave me joy, I gave you doubt! You gave me hope, I gave you despondency! You gave me a second chance! And what did I do with it? What I did with my whole life! I killed! I'm a killer! I should be killed. Locked up till I learn my lesson! (*Desperate.*) I can't learn! I never learned! Never! Never! Never! Don't deny it, Abe, you're a saint! A saint! How could you put up with it? (*Embraces* ABE.) A man's best friend! (*Whips out a pistol.*) Kill me! Shoot me! (ABE *shoots—and misses. He blows a big hole in the back wall. Sunlight pours in.* COHN *and* ABE *squint in the sudden light.* JOAN *is bathed in light. She sits up slowly, rubbing her eyes.* COHN *does not see her. To* ABE.) Idiot! Numbskull! Can't you do anything right? (*Grabs pistol from* ABE *and turns it on himself.*)

JOAN. Cohn!

(JOAN's *cry causes* COHN's *hand to jerk at the moment of fire. A great hole is blown in the side wall. Sunlight pours in.* COHN *whirls on* JOAN, *drops the gun and falls to his knees beside her. He covers his face with his hands and weeps.* JOAN *strokes his head.*)

COHN. A miracle! An angel from heaven!

JOAN. No, it's only me.

COHN. Say you forgive me.

JOAN. For what?

COHN. (*Angry.*) *Never mind for what! Say it!* (*In self-reproach.*) I did it again! (*Starts banging his head.*) Dog! Vermin! Pestilence!

JOAN. (*Gently.*) Cohn— (COHN *looks up.* JOAN *rises from couch, shakily.*) I must leave you.

COHN. What are you saying?

JOAN. Farewell.

COHN. You're too sick to go out. It's freezing out there. Snow. Rain. Sit. Rest.

JOAN. Farewell, Abe.

ABE. More tricks?

COHN. Don't go! I deserve it, but don't!

JOAN. Abe, can you ever forgive me?

ABE. What's to forgive?

JOAN. You hate me.

ABE. Who hates? I'm objective.

JOAN. You're angry with me.

ABE. Anger is a waste. I'm objective.

JOAN. You're disappointed in me.

ABE. Disappointment is subjective. I'm objective.

JOAN. Abe, I'm sorry. I must go. Something is calling me.

COHN. Nothing! What? Something?

JOAN. —something inside—

COHN. Calling you?

JOAN. Inside. Something.

COHN. Voices?

JOAN. No. Yes! Voices! Oh, Cohn, how did you know?

COHN. I have to hear!

JOAN. How can you hear what's inside me?

COHN. Don't cut me out, Joan! I'm a dying man.

JOAN. I'm a dying woman.

COHN. Don't compete. (*Puts his head against her belly.*) Let me hear! Tell them it's me! Cohn! *Voices!* Name it! Cohn does it! No more kidding around.

JOAN. (*Tries to break away.*) I must go.

COHN. (*Holds her.*) It's not fair! (*They struggle.*)

JOAN. (*Begins to stagger.*) You must let me—

COHN. Voices! (JOAN *topples over.* COHN *catches her in his arms.*) What is this? (*To* ABE.) What's the matter with her?

ABE. You did it again.

COHN. Joan. Don't joke, Joan. (*Drags her into the light.*) You want to go? Is that it? Is that all you want? You're free. Free as a bird. Go. Go, Joan. Go. (*Drags her to hole in the wall.*) You're free. Did I say no? Wake up, Joan. Go. Go! Go! (*To* ABE.) She won't go.

ABE. She's dead.

COHN. She won't go. See? I'm holding her loose. What can I do? It's her decision. Look how loose I'm holding her. (JOAN *rises out of* COHN'S *arms and floats high above his head.*)

JOAN Farewell!

COHN. You'll hurt yourself!

JOAN. I am off.

COHN. Without me?!

JOAN. I'm off to heaven. Happiness is waiting. Fields of green, sunlight—

COHN. You can't get there that way! You need a rocket ship! You told me so yourself!

JOAN. Not if you're dead.

COHN. You're not dead.

JOAN. I am dead.

COHN. No! I deny it!

ABE. Stop arguing! Can't you see she's dead?

COHN. If she's dead, why is she up there?

ABE. If she's alive, *how* did she get up thére? Bow your head. A little respect.

COHN. (*Cannot bow his head.*) How can I not see her for the last time?

JOAN. I am going far but I have come far. I have been several people, seen terrible things, had my heart broken then spliced, have been shot at—

COHN. No!

JOAN. —have escaped, have been trapped, have escaped, have found God and lost him, found hope, lost it, grown weak, grown ill, passed out, recovered, walked on water, performed miracles, died, and floated up to the ceiling. And out of these myriad experiences I have learned all that I know and this is the sum of it: I have learned that however prosperous you should get out of the house, however satisfied you should be dissatisfied, however disillusioned you need hope, however hopeless you need patience, however impatient you need dignity, however dignified you need to relax, however relaxed you need rage, however enraged you need love, however loved you need a sense of proportion, however dispassionate you need passion, however possessive you need friends, however many friends you need privacy, however private you need to eat, however well-fed you need books, however well-read you need trials, however tried you need truth and with truth goes trust and with trust goes certainty and with certainty goes calm and with calm goes cool and with cool goes collected but not so cool and collected you can't be hot and bothered. And if you're hot you need affection and if you're affectionate you want perfection, but however imperfect you needn't complain all the time. However lost you need to be found, however found you need to change, however changed you need simplicity, however simple, not *too* simple or oversimple, however righteous not self-righteous, however conscious not self-conscious or self-hating or self-seeking, but you should be self-sufficient, but not alienated, not despair-

ing, not sneering, not cynical, not clinical, not dead
unless you are dead and even then make the most of
it. As I hope to do now. But first: My Last Will and
Testament.

COHN. No!

JOAN. You must hear me.

COHN. It's not true!

ABE. (*To* COHN.) Now at the end a little respect.

JOAN. To Abe I bequeath my armor in the hope of
inspiring strong resolve and the courage to find a con-
viction. To Cohn I bequeath my Voices because he
needs all the help he can get.

FIRST VOICE. I won't go!

SECOND VOICE. I object!

(COHN, *in amazement, looks down at his stomach.*)

WISEMAN. (*Leaps up from his napping place and
bangs gavel.*) Objection overruled. Case dismissed.
(*Scoops up* JOAN'S *armor and runs for the hole in the
back wall.*)

ABE. (*Starts after him.*) That's my armor!

WISEMAN. Miarma? That's in Florida! (*He leaps
out of the hole.* ABE *leaps after him. Both disappear
from view. Sounds of a terrific struggle.*)

COHN. (*Stumbles.*) Who's pushing me?

FIRST VOICE. Him.

SECOND VOICE. It's you I'm pushing, not Cohn.

COHN. (*Stumbles.*) Well, quit pushing.

FIRST VOICE. Well, you tell him to quit pushing.

COHN. (*He stumbles backwards.*) Cut it out!

SECOND VOICE. You heard him.

FIRST VOICE. He meant you!

SECOND VOICE. You started it.

COHN. You didn't behave this way with Joan!

FIRST VOICE. We're influenced by our environment.

ABE. (*Rises into view, dressed in* JOAN'S *armor, her*

sword raised in victory.) Onward! (*Sword high, he stalks out of sight.*)

COHN. (*Runs to hole in wall.*) Abe! It's pouring! You'll catch your death of cold! Viral pneumonia! A stroke! (*Suddenly stumbles toward hole.*)

SECOND VOICE. Quit shoving!

(COHN, *struggling to stay erect, loses the struggle and tumbles backward through the hole, disappearing from view.*)

FIRST VOICE. Now you did it!

SECOND VOICE Who did it?

FIRST VOICE. I didn't.

SECOND VOICE. No. You're the innocent one around here.

COHN. (*He rises into view, blinking in the strong sunlight.*) It's not as bad as it looks. (*Holds out a hand.*) It's only a drizzle.

FIRST VOICE. It's getting better.

SECOND VOICE. By whose evidence?

FIRST VOICE. The evidence of my senses.

SECOND VOICE. Your senses should have their head examined.

COHN. Shut up. Follow me. (*He walks off.*)

(*Lights fade on* JOAN *frozen in space, apparently heaven-bound.*)

CURTAIN

PROPERTY LIST

PRESET—ACT ONE:

By Fireplace:
 Newspapers to R.
 Fireplace Tools L. (poker D. S.)

On Typewriter Table (From L. to R.):
 Typewriter with typed page
 Ream of paper

On paper/collage
 A few Magazines
 A Saturday Review
 A pair of scissors
 An open bottle of glue
 (NOTE: All items on the table should be pushed back
 as far as possible—)

On Rocking Chair:
 Violin Case
 Violin, upright against back of chair, on violin case
 Music Stand with music and bow above rocker

At Arm Chair:
 Downstage, a standing ashtray with four wooden matches
 Unwrapped, fresh cigar

On Bookcase Ledge:
 On the S. R. Corner a book with Aladdin's lamp on top
  (*Note:* handle to S. L. side)

Around Potbellied Stove:
 D. S., on windowseat is the puzzle
  two red pieces of the puzzle out to be put back
  magnifying glass on top of two red pieces
 Underneath, a box with matches
  a match set sticking out of the box
 In the lower vent, an unwrapped/fresh cigar sticking out,
  two inches

On floor, D. S. of couch
 Misc. books and magazines at head of couch
 One copy of Trotsky book at head of couch

65

Inside Trunk:
Loaded shotgun

On Kitchen Table:
Ashtray with cigar and one match

On Kitchen Stove:
Teapot, full of water, D. S. L. burner
Large pot with lid, containing stew, D. S. R. burner
Flat pan, sprayed with cooking oil, U. R. burner

On top of stove shelf:
small pot, U. L.
salt and pepper, C.
3 pot holders, D. L.
plastic dishes, D. R.
wooden spoon and ladel, on top of pot holders
coffee pot, with 6 oz. of coffee, U. R.

Inside oven:
plate of hors d'oeuvres of Act Two
veal loaf for Act Two

The Refrigerator:
Top shelf:
assortment of canned goods on D. S. side
D. L. parsley on tray
milk carton U. R.
plate with two eggs and fork U. R. C.
plate with chunk of cheese with wax left on D. R.
Bottom Shelf:
rock for Act Two
wrapped chicken leg
full bottle of white wine
fresh carrot with green foliage in front
On top of Refrigerator:
misc. magazines
bucket U. R.
radio U. L.
old fan D. R.
roll of paper towels
On handle:
dish towel (dirty)

On hand rail (above the refrigerator):
Guest book, dusted with talcum powder

On the counter D. S. *or refrigerator:*
  Wine rack
  Cloth Napkins
  Cutting Board
  Knife
  Drain Board
    sets of silverware R. in drain board
    extra silverware
  red wine
  brandy
  scotch
  shot glass
  old fashioned toaster

Under the counter:
  Vial of white power for Act Two (goes in violin case)
  Stainless steel tub for striking dishes at end of Act One

On Shelf above counter and sink:
  Miscellaneous pots and pants set to fall in Act Three

On shelves between Stove and Refrigerator:
  top shelf, D. S.—U. S.
    miscellaneous food and boxes to center—check spaghetti
      supply
    bowls for stew (6)
    wine glasses (6)
    flat plates (4)
  bottom shelf
    more food and boxes
    pitcher full of water to pour in pots in Act Three

On stool:
  Cookbook
  Two/thirds glass of scotch

Set Dressing in Attic (some to fall):
  old TV sets
  rug beaters
  old clocks
  ship models
  wicker baskets
  bird cages
  etc.

Set Before Act One—Offstage Props

On table between Abe and Cohn's bedrooms:
   Stethoscope (Act Three)
   Cotton (Act Three)
   Alcohol (Act Three)
   School Bell (Act Three)
   Large Scissors (Act Three)
   Gavel (Act Three)

In box below Sugarglass Pane:
   Rock with writing (Act Two)

On Table near Railings at Bedrooms:
   Coffee cup and saucer (Act Two)

To the Left of Abe's Bedroom Door in Box:
   Box of Stogie's (All Acts)
   Melville Book (Act One)

At Backstage near Bedrooms:
   Abe's Suitcase (Act Two)

Behind Bookcase:
   On wall:
      Wiseman's clipboard with pen
      The paper is a computer readout that folds along perferations

At Front Door:
   At Left
      White Flag (Act Two)
      Rock for Messenger in box on wall (Act Two)
      Notepad and Quill pen for Messenger on wall (Act Two)

At Backstage Prop Table:
   Dirty Dish prop (Act Three)

Set Act Three—Offstage

On table near railings:
   One-half glass milk (Act Three)

Back in respective boxes:
   All rocks

Back behind bedrooms:
   Suitcase
       A Word of Note—Check in Gamblers coat for *trick cards* and *planned deck* in this order: 10-K-Q-J
       A spade-7 cards —10-J-Q-K-*Double Middle card*
       A spade-K-Q-J-10—7 cards—5 cards—4 red aces.

Act II—Strike Reset

By Fireplace:
  Replace poker L.

On Typewriter Table:
  Strike:
    Guest Book
    Top Revolver

On Rocking Chair:
  Strike:
    Violin case
    Violin

At Armchair:
  Strike:
    Melville Book (Replace back stage)

On Ledge Above Armchair:
  Replace—Aladdin's lamp behind books

Around Heat Stove:
  Strike:
    Puzzle
    Magnifying glass (Replace back stage)
    Aladdin's lamp (See ledge)

On the Couch:
  Strike:
    All magazines

  Replace:
    Blanket
    Violin

On the Table:
  Strike:
    all but one cigar

On the cooking stove:
  Place:
    Coffee pot on D. L. burner
    Veal loaf (lower oven)
    Hors d'oeuvres (upper oven)

Act III—Strike Reset

By Fireplace:
Same

On typewriter Table:
Strike: (*Set*—blank pistol in table)
everything Offstage

On Rocking Chair:
Nothing

At Armchair:
Nothing

On Ledge Above Armchair:
Same

Around Heat Stove:
Nothing

On the Couch:
Nothing

On the Table:
Strike:

Veal loaf
Cigar and lemon drop

Set:

A third place setting
Three wineglasses
Bottle of red wine
Three plates
Salt and pepper

On the Cooking Stove:
Strike:

Coffee Pot

Set:

Large pot three-quarters filled with water and Cauliflower
and green D. L. burner
Small pot R. of large pot also filled with water and potatoes
U. L. burner
Set under plastic dishes and dish towel
Set in the upper oven the Pig with an apple in it's mouth

The Refrigerator:
  Set:
    Chicken leg on the upper shelf
    (6 oz.) glass of milk half full (*Off Right*)

On the Counter:
  Put into dish drainer dish:
    Cutting board and knife
    Cloth napkins

  Set:
    Bring the shot glass and decanter forward
    The dirt prop
    The black pan and the ladle on top of the dirt prop

Under the Counter:
  Strike:
    Violin case
    Vial

Shelf above the sink:
  Same

Shelves between Stove and Sink:
  Same

On Stool:
  Set:
    Cookbook (Open)
    Stack of dishes

> BE SURE PORK RIND IS NEXT TO PIG

COSTUME PLOT

ABE:

COSTUME No. 1—ACT ONE:
Red striped shirt
Suspenders
Silk scarf
Dark red robe
Grey flannel trousers
Black sox
Black slippers
Tortoise shell glasses

COSTUME No. 2—ACT TWO:
Tattersall shirt
Grey flannel trousers (same)
Black sox (same)
Blue canvas shoes (same)
Suspenders (same)
Glasses (same)
Maroon smoking jacket (pre-set, back stage)
Blue sweater vest (pre-set, back stage)

Add:
Blue canvas coat (pre-set, back stage)
Turquoise and purple scarves (pre-set, back stage)
Green canvas hat (pre-set, back stage)
Red ear muffs (pre-set, back stage)
Black homburg hat (preset, back stage)
Black golashes (pre-set, back stage)
Leather mittens (preset, back stage)

COSTUME No. 3—ACT THREE:
Grey tweed trousers
Beige shirt
Camel sweater vest
Rust paisley tie
Blue canvas shoes (same)
Black sox (same)

Add:
Helmet (pre-set, on stage)
Breast Plate (pre-set, back stage)
Gauntlets (pre-set, back stage)

COHN:

Costume No. 1—Act One:
Wool plaid shirt
Brown corduroy pants
Green cardigan
Brown argyle sox
Brown slip-on shoes

Costume No. 2:
Brown pants (same)
Brown sox (same)
Brown shoes (same)
Tattered shirt (pre-set, back stage)
Tattered sweater (pre-set, back stage)

Costume No. 3:
Brown pants (same)
Brown sox (same)
Brown shoes (same)
Black and red plaid shirt (pre-set, back stage)

Costume No. 4—Act Two:
Blue corduroy pants
Orange shirt
Wool cardigan vest
Suspenders
Brown shoes (same)
Black sox

Costume No. 5—Act Three:
Blue Corduroy pants
Suspenders
Plaid flannel shirt
Brown shoes (same)
Black sox (same)

WISEMAN:

> COSTUME NO. 1—ACT ONE:
>   White shirt
>   Tie
>   Black pinstripe 3 pc. suit
>   Black sox
>   Black boots
>   *Add:*
>   White robe (pre-set, on stage)
>   Beard (pre-set, on stage)
>   Turban (pre-set, back stage)

MESSENGER:

> COSTUME NO. 2:
>   Uniform jacket
>   Uniform pants
>   Hat with attached hair
>   Glasses
>   Mustache and eyebrows
>   Black shoes (same)
>   Black sox (same)

SOLDIER:

> COSTUME:
>   Army jacket
>   Army pants
>   Gas mask and pouch
>   Helmet
>   Boots
>   Sox

GAMBLER:

> COSTUME NO. 3—ACT TWO:
>   White shirt, tie and vest (rigged together)
>   White coat
>   White trousers
>   Mustache
>   Black sox (same)
>   Black boots (same)
>   White robe (same) with star

JUDGE:

Costume No. 4—Act Three:
Black 3 pc. suit (same)
White shirt (same)
Black tie
Black robe
Glasses
Beard (same)

JOAN:

Costume No. 1—Act One, Two:
Helmet with plume
Breastplate
Gauntlets
Grieves
Arm pieces
White skirt
Chain mail tights
Chain mail T-shirt
Grey leotards
Grey tights
Chain mail cowl
Sword
Silver shoes

Costume No. 2:
Flying harness
Brown dress with apron
Petticoats
Brown tights
Black shoes
Bandanna (hair back)

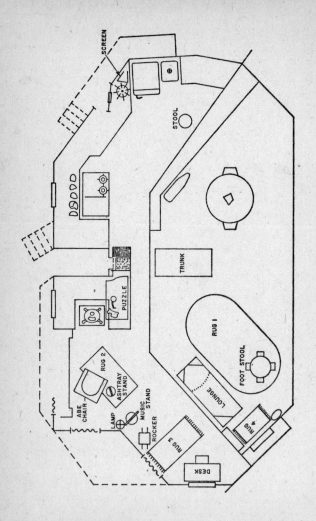

SCREEN

STOOL

TRUNK

STOOL

RUG 1

FOOT STOOL

LOUNGE

RUG 4

PUZZLE

RUG 2

ASHTRAY STAND

ABE CHAIR

LAMP

MUSIC STAND

ROCKER

RUG 3

DESK

GROUND PLAN KNOCK KNOCK   ACT I

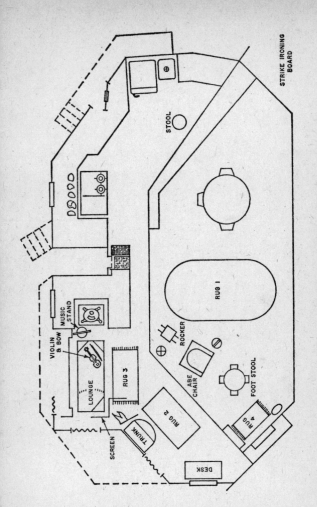

GROUND PLAN KNOCK KNOCK   ACT II

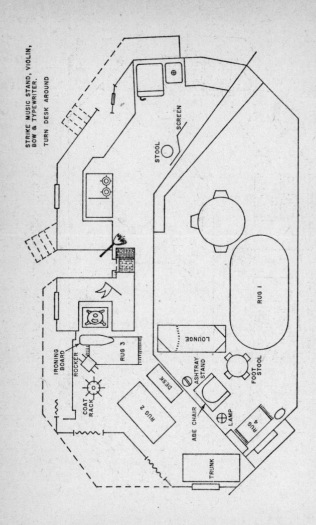

STRIKE MUSIC STAND, VIOLIN,
BOW & TYPEWRITER.

TURN DESK AROUND

GROUND PLAN KNOCK KNOCK   ACT III

The Gingerbread Lady

NEIL SIMON
(Little Theatre) Comedy-Drama
3 Men, 3 Women—Interior

Maureen Stapleton played the Broadway part of a popular singer who has gone to pot with booze and sex. We meet her at the end of a ten-week drying out period at a sanitarium, when her friend, her daughter, and an actor try to help her adjust to sobriety. But all three have the opposite effect on her. The friend is so constantly vain she loses her husband; the actor, a homosexual, is also doomed, and indeed loses his part three days before an opening; and the daughter needs more affection than she can spare her mother. Enter also a former lover louse, who ends up giving her a black eye. The birthday party washes out, the gingerbread lady falls off the wagon and careens onward to her own tragic end.

"He has combined an amusing comedy with the atmosphere of great sadness. His characteristic wit and humor are at their brilliant best, and his serious story of lost misfits can often be genuinely and deeply touching."—N.Y. Post. "Contains some of the brightest dialogue Simon has yet composed."—N.Y. Daily News. "Mr. Simon's play is as funny as ever—the customary avalanche of hilarity, and landslide of pure unbuttoned joy . . . Mr. Simon is a funny, funny man—with tears running down his cheek."—N.Y. Times.

Royalty $50-$35

The Sunshine Boys

NEIL SIMON
(All Groups) Comedy
5 Men, 2 Women

An ex-vaudeville team, Al Lewis and Willie Clarke, in spite of playing together for forty-three years, have a natural antipathy for one another. (Willie resents Al's habit of poking a finger in his chest, or perhaps accidentally spitting in his face). It has been eleven years since they have performed together, when along comes CBS-TV, who is preparing a "History of Comedy" special, that will of course include Willie and Al—the "Lewis and Clark" team back together again. In the meantime, Willie has been doing spot commercials, like for Schick (the razor blade shakes) or for Frito-Lay potato chips (he forgets the name), while Al is happily retired. The team gets back together again, only to have Al poke his finger in Willie's chest, and accidentally spit in his face.

". . . the most delightful play Mr. Simon has written for several seasons and proves why he is the ablest current author of stage humor."—Watts, N. Y. Post. "None of Simon's comedies has been more intimately written out of love and a bone-deep affinity with the theatrical scene and temperament." Time. ". . . another hit for Neil Simon in this shrewdly balanced, splendidly performed and rather touching slice of the show-biz life."—Watt, New York Daily News. "(Simon) . . . writes the most dependably crisp and funny dialogue around . . . always well-set and polished to a high lustre."—WABC-TV. ". . . a vaudeville act within a vaudeville act . . . Simon has done it again."—WCBS-TV.

Royalty $50-$35

#20

6 RMS RIV VU

BOB RANDALL

(Little Theatre) Comedy

4 Men, 4 Women, Interior

A vacant apartment with a river view is open for inspection by prospective tenants, and among them are a man and a woman who have never met before. They are the last to leave and, when they get ready to depart, they find that the door is locked and they are shut in. Since they are attractive young people, they find each other interesting and the fact that both are happily married adds to their delight of mutual, yet obviously separate interests.

"... a Broadway comedy of fun and class, as cheerful as a rising souffle. A sprightly, happy comedy of charm and humor. Two people playing out a very vital game of love, an attractive fantasy with a precious tincture of truth to it."— *N.Y. Times.*
"... perfectly charming entertainment, sexy, romantic and funny."—*Women's Wear Daily.*

Royalty, $50–$35

WHO KILLED SANTA CLAUS?

TERENCE FEELY

(All Groups) Thriller

6 Men, 2 Women, Interior

Barbara Love is a popular television 'auntie'. It is Christmas, and a number of men connected with her are coming to a party. Her secretary, Connie, is also there. Before they arrive she is threatened by a disguised voice on her Ansaphone, and is sent a grotesque 'murdered' doll in a coffin, wearing a dress resembling one of her own. She calls the police, and a handsome detective arrives. Shortly afterwards her guests follow. It becomes apparent that one of those guests is planning to kill her. Or is it the strange young man who turns up unexpectedly, claiming to belong to the publicity department, but unknown to any of the others?

"... is a thriller with heaps of suspense, surprises, and nattily cleaver turns and twists ... Mr. Feeley is technically highly skilled in the artificial range of operations, and his dialogue is brilliantly effective."—The Stage. London.

Royalty, $50–$25